LEAD YOU

DOWNLOAD YOUR FREE GIFTS

Read This First

Just to say thanks for buying and reading my book,
I would like to give you a few free bonus gifts,
no strings attached.

To download now, visit
www.leadyoubook.com/Freegifts

BOBBY HARRINGTON

LEAD YOU

THE WINNING COMBINATION TO ACHIEVE PERSONAL AND PROFESSIONAL SUCCESS

LEAD YOU

The Winning Combination to Achieve Personal and Professional Success

ISBN 978-1-5445-3624-8 Hardcover
978-1-5445-3625-5 Paperback
978-1-5445-3626-2 Ebook

For my wife Angella

and children, Laura Lee, and Ethan.

You gave me the wind to fill my sails

during rough seas and

dark hours.

CONTENTS

INTRODUCTION

Imagine a person presented with an opportunity to lead others or make a critical decision, and at the moment of truth, they could not make it happen. They sit and wonder why they failed to launch. They worked hard and put in the time and effort, yet something is missing, and they are not standing out from the crowd. They ask themselves, *Why is this happening to me?* Likewise, they struggle emotionally to make sense of it. The inability to lead or make a sound decision may have resulted in a setback.

To make matters worse, now they have to figure out why they did not launch in addition to managing the setback. The person has the potential to take charge of his dream and life, but he cannot find the answer. The answer to his question lies within himself and who he is.

Why are you failing at leading others? The answer is simple: you are not leading yourself first. Why do some people lead themselves better than others? This answer is also simple: people who lead themselves effectively know the leadership basics, execute with passion and discipline, and commit to continuous improvement. The information in this book provides perspectives and tools that empower you to lead yourself effectively. Let's discuss the reasons you should invest time in reading this book.

People who poorly lead themselves lack an awareness of leadership traits, values, and the concept that we must **lead ourselves first** before we can lead others. They have failed at personal accountability and responsibility, which stems from the lack of leadership traits and personal values cultivation. They are not living their values; instead, they follow the status quo. They are limiting potential and stagnate because they have no self-leadership awareness. They are not putting in the work because they do not know how. Without awareness and adoption of a self-leadership structure, people cannot cultivate and continuously improve how they lead themselves, which results in frustration, setbacks, loss of personal relationships, and bad behavior. People are not getting what they want because *they* are the obstacle. The good news is that with awareness, tools, and hard work, people can turn it around and improve their self-leadership.

Transform Your Idea of Self-Leadership to Transform Your Life

Adopting a self-leadership framework and putting in the hard work provides an opportunity to transform people into the leaders they aspire to be. You do not have to be the same person tomorrow as you were today. After taking personal inventory and having a hard and honest conversation with yourself, you can begin to transform your life by leading yourself first. Improvements in your personal, interpersonal, family, and business are assured. You will become a more confident, self-assured, and informed individual. People will notice and appreciate your willingness to change for the better. Your ability to change is only limited by your willingness to do the hard work. And the hard work you put into your transformation makes for lasting positive changes in your life. No one can change us; it is a personal choice to change.

There are countless benefits to leading yourself first. Deciding to commit to a leadership framework solves the self-leadership misunderstanding as you no longer wonder what it takes to lead yourself well. When people lead themselves effectively, they are more productive, constructive, and promotable. Everyone would like to be more productive in their personal and work life. Likewise, we all prefer constructive interactions and relationships at home and at work.

Who does not want better relationships? Personal and career promotion are almost certain for people who work hard at improving their self-leadership. Even when setbacks occur, people who understand how to lead themselves effectively recover faster and use the setback as a learning opportunity. The benefit of managing setbacks cannot be overstated.

Moreover, the Lead You method is an easy-to-follow leadership framework. Complicated leadership theories and blueprints are not sustainable. People need and want a simple guide to improve their self-leadership. Lead You provides a simple guide for maximum benefit. Like personal character, everyone develops a leadership character. This text provides the benefit of a road map to achieve your individual leadership character.

Lead You applies a building block approach coupled with real-life antidotes and perspectives on self-leadership. The book provides an opportunity to learn a self-leadership framework. It provides the basic building blocks critical for long-term personal and professional growth and success.

In Chapters 1 through 5, I will lay out the foundations of the self-leadership framework and discuss how it results in leadership character. In Chapters 6 and 7, I will pivot to self-trust, self-belief, commitment, and discipline and underpin personal responsibility. You will learn the critical understanding that trust and belief in self, commitment, and discipline are interconnected. In Chapters 8–12, I will cover sovereignty, the career dilemma, perfection, and self-care.

You will learn the concept of sovereignty and how it applies to personal leadership. I will discuss the various approaches to a career and how your job is the best way to succeed. Moreover, you will learn a realistic and new perspective of how the perfect concept fits and does not fit into leadership. Failure is certain;

how we deal with failure determines growth and success and our ability to do the most important thing a leader can do—keep moving. I will walk you through this and show you how to get the results. Lastly, I will discuss why it is essential to maintain a good sense of self-care.

I have spent thirty-four years of servanthood leadership in sports, martial arts, the military, private business, and a Fortune/Global 100 company. During my work career, I have held positions as an individual contributor, subject-matter expert, team leader, technologist, advisor, supervisor, and manager. No matter the title, I always leaned on self-leadership, and I have considered it a privilege to lead others. I have been a student of leaders and leadership my whole life, and leadership in its many permutations has always interested me. The information in this book stems from my leadership experiences and tools learned at home, in the US Marine Corps, and along my thirty-four-year leadership journey.

More importantly, I had a personal transformation six years ago and revisited the self-leadership basics articulated in this book. It helped me through a difficult time, and I know it can help you too. My single mission is to improve you.

This book **is** a real-world, practical self-leadership framework that is easy to use and understand. The book **is not** a high-level, confusing dissertation on leadership theory. I trust you will find it simple and usable. I challenge you to improve yourself, and I am willing and able to help you.

Lead You is for **you,** the person who has the determination to improve. Are you ready to have an honest conversation with yourself and learn what it takes so you can become the empowered leader you dream of being? Keep reading.

CHAPTER 1

THE MOST IMPORTANT CONVERSATION

The most important conversation you will ever have is the one you have with yourself. It took me forty-five years of accomplishment, failure, and struggle to finally have mine. The internal conversation begins with a trigger, an event, a provocative thought, circumstances, desire, and the like. The trigger point represents a moment where we feel that there is no runway left; we need help. It is different for everyone.

My trigger happened at work after a challenging three-year work assignment. I already had a few of these moments in my life—washing out of college football, leaving the Marine Corps, small business bankruptcy—yet, none had this kind of tone. I believe it was because I was forty-five years old, and in my mind, I was halfway through life, so I felt I should have had firm control of everything in my life. Yet, I was far from where I wanted to be at the time.

In 2012, I left an oil refinery to work in the upstream oil and gas sector, where the main objective was to extract and produce oil and gas from the earth. Although structured, the upstream environment is more of a figure-it-out-as-you-go operation versus an oil refinery's refined and dialed-in operations. As a result, I struggled in the first fourteen months of the assignment.

I had been a people leader for over twenty-two years—spanning the military, private business, contracting, and seven years in a Fortune 100 company. In addition, I had been to war, owned my own business, and had just spent eight years developing technology that saved my employer millions of dollars. Likewise, I was well versed in technical and people leadership. I was used to being a top performer no matter what environment I was in at the time.

My time in the United States Marine Corps, private business, and eight years developing and implementing technology represented meaningful experience and leadership assignments of increasing responsibility. I was used to working in isolation, but this 28-on/28-off work schedule was different. The 28/28 schedule requires you to work in a foreign business unit for twenty-eight days; then, you take time off for twenty-eight days.

In a nutshell, you spend six months at work and six months at home. It was balls to the wall for twenty-eight days straight while onsite at work.

I worked hard as a contributor and a leader my whole life. Max fucking effort. So, at this point, I should have been seasoned and ready to take on any challenge. Dead wrong. In a sense, I had failed to launch. There are too many factors to cite, so I will just say I was overwhelmed, and for the first time in my life, I started to look in the mirror and question my competence. I knew I had what it took, but I needed to answer some questions about myself before I could figure it out.

Chaos and Struggle Are Teachers

Chaos defined the new work environment, and I was unprepared for it. Every day, there were red faces in meetings and one-on-one conversations in the work environment. It was that kind of place. I remember my boss was ordered to go back to his room and lie down after a profanity-laced tirade when someone from operations assigned blame to our group. That was an omen. The site leadership was poor in some areas, and they chose to remedy conflict by asking folks to go to their room and cool off instead of managing the conflict. De-escalation and cooling periods are helpful conflict management tools; however, sending folks to their room became a camp legend and fodder.

Likewise, people did not care about my track record when I arrived at my new assignment. I was adept at earning respect, but I did not expect little to any respect when I arrived. It is not like I showed up and thought I was big shit; on the contrary, I still despised those types of people. I had an accomplished track record in my field and put in twenty years of hard work in my discipline.

Not long into the new assignment, I struggled to maintain healthy relationships, influence, and get along with my bosses. Building relationships, influence, and getting along with the boss were strengths in my past assignments, so what was the root cause of the problem? How could I possibly be struggling with my strengths? For months, the thought reeled in my head. The thing is, no one was any wiser about my struggles. I had always done a good job of bottling things up and pushing down trauma and personal issues. I did not ask for much help from others as I always thought it was a crutch. I learned to figure out things on my own for the most part.

Sleeping with the Big-Ass Rat

To make matters worse, I could not get into the company accommodations in camp because of a union strike. The unions are powerful in Nigeria, and they control a significant part of the workforce. I was assigned a filthy room with a leaking ceiling—not so much fun in the rainy season when you are trying to do pushups in half an inch of water. Additionally, rats and roaches infested the room. I am not talking about a mouse you see in your house or the pet store. The rats in the camp are as giant as small cats. The big-ass rat (BAR) shit on my toilet seat every night. The carpet was full of rat piss, so when you bottomed out on a pushup, there was a big whiff of piss.

In the Marine Corps, they trained us to fight, kill, and butcher in all types of conditions—clean, dirty, and anywhere in between—and expected us to thrive no matter what. Improvise, adapt, overcome. No problem. The Marines never, and I mean never, had dirty/filthy accommodations. Cleaning is one of the first skills developed in the Marine Corps. When assigned a space, you clean it. When you arrive at a new squad bay, you tend it—getting the picture? I cleaned the room the best I could, but I could not control all the conditions or the BAR. The net effect of the BAR on me was little sleep leading to the breakdown of patience, bearing, and sometimes decision-making. It was like the bouts of extreme insomnia I had dealt with years earlier after the Corps.

A New Perspective

I never read much, as I got bored of books quickly, especially if I sensed driveling, and I do not like others doing the thinking for me. There were exceptions if the content kept me interested. I did have a few books on leadership and biographies because people interest me, and I have studied leadership since my days in the Marine Corps. One night as I was reading the book *Lone Survivor*, the answer to my struggle came to me with clarity. Marcus Luttrell fell down the mountain in Afghanistan a few times and fought until he had nothing left. He did not give up and did his absolute best in the worst situations. While I have never given up, I was not leading myself effectively, and I was not giving my *absolute* best at work or in other areas of my life. I was working hard; however, that was not good enough. More effort and different behaviors were required to succeed.

Likewise, the revelation of my effort caused me to examine other parts of my life. My life was okay, or so I thought, in terms of family, belief system, finances, and health. Still, I felt unfulfilled and fell short of my outright best. I was living the status quo. I had a handsome salary, was overweight, had money but no real financial plan, and did not nurture my family relationships. I uncovered areas that I needed to work on in my marriage. I was trying to win every conversation instead of winning the relationship. Petty arguments became mushroom clouds—*War of the Roses* stuff. Also, the distance created a strain and additional challenge on my marriage and family relationships.

After a while, the family was desensitized to me leaving every four weeks. It got to the point where I felt I was intruding on their lives when I returned home. It is a hard fact to accept, but it happens. I would easily get frustrated with my teenage children, which is not a good recipe for conflict management. A few times, I had to ask myself, who is the adult and who is the child here?

I realized I had reduced myself to a provider instead of being a leader and mentor as I had been before. I have never been one for ideology or theology; however, I am deeply spiritual. Somehow, I lost belief in everything. Worse yet, I had lost belief in myself. In my assessment, I had become selfish, and I did not live up to personal accountability standards.

Later, around 2016, I came across another book named *Extreme Ownership* by Seal Team Officers Jocko Willink and Leif Babin. The book articulates the leadership and teamwork concepts used in the 2006 combat operations of Task Unit Bruiser in Iraq. The main takeaway for me was to take ownership of everything.

While I had learned and practiced that leaders are ultimately accountable, the concept of extreme ownership is proactive and a broader call to action. I could relate to the leadership traits and principles expressed in the book. I particularly gravitated and tracked with the lessons on making decisions amid uncertainty. Stay calm, look around, and "make a decision" is the mantra. In my new role, I was not going to get all the information I needed, so being decisive in decision-making—right or wrong—was the best course of action. The book further reinforced my need to return to the leadership structure I had learned years earlier.

There is a significant difference between just getting it done and doing your best, striving for excellence. I was doing well; however, I was not doing as well as I knew I could. After this sobering self-revelation, I started to reflect and ask questions of myself, and I arrived at that genuine, sunk-in burning chest feeling of shame and guilt. I was not leading myself effectively, and I had let myself down because I did not do my absolute best.

It was a cut-the-crap and get-real moment. Usually, others made me feel this way instead of myself. I knew this type of self-talk would be different, and it had to be honest. There was nowhere to run, no talking myself out of it, no profuse explaining, and no blaming others. It was time to own everything. I was the only person who was going to fix me.

Getting Real and Raw

I started a brutally honest internal evaluation. The evaluation turned into a conversation, and I would spend each night of the remaining twenty-eight-day rotation in deep talk. Looking back on that period, I realize it was the most important conversation I ever had as a leader. I would not have recovered and made it this far if it were not for that internal dialogue. This new conversation was different from everyday self-talk. As I like to say, it was a "heavy" conversation. The more honest I got, the deeper the questions became. Why is this happening? What do I do?

What is it going to take to get there? Where do I start? What pain have I caused others? What does it take to recover?

Looking in the Mirror

The most important conversation we have as leaders is one with ourselves. I have always noticed that I have had an inner voice—a narrator—and a way to organize my thoughts. Some describe this as an inner monologue. What is the value of having an internal conversation—essentially, a conversation with yourself?

Having a conversation with yourself is the same as asking outward for help. It is an acknowledgment that help is needed. The difference between self-talk and talking to others is that we cannot lie to ourselves, gloss over facts, or deny issues. We have 100 percent of the relevant knowledge regarding our problems.

Carrying around mental issues and problems for too long is like trying to physically move around a hundred-pound bag. Sooner or later, you cannot possibly carry on—or you get hurt.

So what subject matter should the internal conversation contain? I am simple, so I asked myself, *Why did this happen? What does it mean? How did I get here? What do I need to do to right the ship?* Notice that the questions are inward-facing. How did I? What did I? No more assigning blame and looking outward. I had to start doing the work; I had to own everything. And that is what I did.

As I assessed my behaviors and actions against the leadership traits and principles learned decades earlier, I realized that I fell short of meeting, let alone exceeding, those standards. Standards are the way to measure performance. So, I committed to systematically taking an inventory of all the areas in my life and returning wholeheartedly to the standards I learned at home, in the US Marine Corps, and in my leadership journey. But first, I had to earn back my self-trust and believe in myself again.

I did not live up to the standards I had been raised with and the ones I had adopted over the course of my life. Self-trust is only developed by keeping promises to yourself and living to and exceeding your own standards. Earning trust from others is difficult; earning back broken trust from oneself is harder. Breaking trust is serious. Trust is like building a structure (a house or an office building)—it takes months or years to make and minutes to destroy; it is hard to acquire and easy to lose.

Hard Assignments Reveal Our Ability

There is a well-known saying: "a rising tide lifts all boats." The correlation is that what is good for one is good for all. The same holds for leadership. In a business environment where the budget and the organizational structures are sound and resources are abundant, everyone can shine as a leader. Conversely, when the budget is limited, the talent pool is small and unqualified, and you build a team from minimal working parts, you will realize that chaos and challenge expose weaknesses quickly for the most seasoned leadership practitioners. This is good. The key is recognizing that exposing one's flaws is a gift and invaluable feedback. It is a beautiful thing because it is an opportunity to improve and develop resilience.

People say knowledge is power. Maybe. I would argue that perspective is power. We are empowered and stronger self-leaders when we allow ourselves to develop and accept alternate perspectives. When we recognize our flaws, we learn to see the same in others, making us influential coaches, mentors, and leaders. When we see our own best attributes, we see them in others.

Accepting and developing alternative perspectives is a win-win proposition. Accumulating different perspectives along the journey in life takes us to the mountaintop, and it takes a mountaintop perspective to translate it into a habitual way of being.

Every new assignment or position requires a new leader to emerge in you. But more importantly, we must lead ourselves differently too. Circumstances are great antagonists, so we need a full leadership toolbox flush with traits and values. The best way to conquer circumstances is to keep our toolbox at the ready with expert knowledge of each tool. It takes practice, failure, practice, failure, and learning to master traits and values. Joe Montana said, "repetition is king." Such steadfast and immovable wisdom.

Despite the best of circumstances, sometimes we lose our perspective. We get comfortable and believe that we have reached the top of the mountain. The truth is that when it comes to leading ourselves, we never arrive. We all improve every day, and self-leadership requires constant self-evaluation. We will fail, sometimes miserably, even at strengths. There is a reason—usually, we have chosen to go outside our comfort zone. Once you gain mastery of traits and values, you will seldom collapse unless you lose self-control.

Success at one venue does not assure the same at another. Sports is an excellent analogy to this concept. Have you ever seen an "A" player go to a lousy team or a different system? Even the A players must adjust to new environments. It happens, and no one is immune to improvement. At some point, we must look inward and take inventory of our leadership qualities and ability. When I learned to become unselfish and take more personal responsibility, I became a better leader of myself. In turn, I effectively led others. Becoming a better leader started with an unpleasant, honest, internal conversation and inventory of where I needed to improve. I examined areas outside of work, such as family, belief system, financial, and physical fitness dimensions of my life.

I had to acknowledge that I was not perfect and accept that I had developed a pattern over the last few years. The previous eight years of fail, fail, fail, traction, fail, fail, success had taken a toll. The new assignment knocked me down. I felt like I had left a job that was a high point for me, a real career best, for what turned out to be a shit show.

The worst failure is the one we feel inside. Sure, failing in front of others might be embarrassment or humiliation. That passes, but the feeling of letting yourself down is the absolute worst. It is like trying to scrub off a tattoo with a washcloth. It is not happening quickly. Competitive people see failure as more than not meeting the mark. Failure is a special kind of sting, even if we view it as an opportunity to learn, grow, or rearm. And it should be because folks work hard and want to experience success.

Rock bottom comes in many variations. It is a time when things cannot get any worse in a specific space in life. The most common are financial and drug or alcohol addiction. Emotionally, I was at rock bottom. I would argue that emotional rock bottom trumps all others, although it might accompany other forms of rock bottom. I believe the emptiness found there serves as a prompt to inventory. It certainly caused me to evaluate my situation.

Rock bottom can serve as a platform to count blessings and look for the positives. After all, there are many, no matter the circumstance folks are in at the time. Life above ground, relatively good health, and safety all count as positive and are a reason to count the good things.

I learned many lessons from the three-year assignment in Nigeria. One of the most important ones was to take the time to self-assess and to begin an earnest conversation with myself about the problems I was facing. In my case, self-help began with looking inward before outward. Often, I have seen in people and myself that we already have much, if not all, of what we need to solve our problems. After all, we behaved our way into the issues. Intuitively, we should behave out of the situation. It is not complicated. It does take honesty, courage, and willpower to change. Change does not come easy—it is a struggle.

Moreover, we grow as problem solvers and become independent when we solve our issues. Developing independence helps us navigate the trials of life, is rewarding, and builds confidence. Self-confidence leads to self-belief and self-trust. Self-confidence and self-trust support other positive traits. Like building blocks, self-confidence, self-belief, and confidence build a solid foundation for commitment and discipline. We cover the three attributes in Chapters 6 and 7.

The Payout for Having the Hard Conversation

The benefit of the hard conversation is the payout for working hard to improve. I began to answer and make plans to address the questions that came to me. *Why is this happening?* I was responsible for my digression and no one else. I did not lead myself effectively; therefore, other parts of my life degraded. *What do I do?* I had the honest conversation, and I had to immediately work to understand and start improving in critical areas of my life.

What is it going to take to get there? It was apparent from the start of the improvement plan that there would be hard conversations, and I had to behave my way out of circumstances I had caused. I humbled myself and asked my family the pinpointed questions: *How can I be a better father and husband? Where do I start?* For me, starting with the leadership basics is what worked. I recalibrated with what I had learned before, and, most importantly, I learned to be unselfish.

What pain have I caused others? When I looked back, I had caused my family pain by not being fully present. Likewise, I had engaged in petty arguments that were not constructive. *What does it take to recover?* Recovery from digression is not immediate; it is a journey. After all, when we fall, it will take time to get up and stay consistent. It is critical to write down the questions and chart a course of action to improve.

I have been on a seven-year self-improvement journey. My journey started with an honest conversation, and I converted the output into a course-of-action improvement plan. I did not use the *course-of-action* term when I created the plan, as I learned the term in 2019 while pursuing a bachelors degree in Intelligence Studies and International Relations. However, the term *course of action* is essential. It represents a plan that contributes to mission accomplishment.

The plan included Belief System, Family, Financial Planning, Physical Fitness, and Work. Each area required a critical assessment and analysis to determine where the work was needed. Remember, it is not about maintaining the status quo; we should give our best in these spaces. The status quo is almost as bad as not trying because we are leaving effort and results on the table, and there is no going back to get that day or that opportunity or the growth that comes with doing our best.

When attacking a problem, I am a "root cause" and "cold turkey" kind of person. I believe that addressing symptoms leads to a protracted, corrective action campaign. Rip the Band-Aid off and get to work. I would do the same with the five improvement areas that I identified. I started with family first because everything in my world emanates from my support system, and my family is my only reliable support system. I would have to have hard conversations with myself and my family. Through the conversations and awareness, I became more patient.

Hard Work Produces the Right Results

Over the last seven years, I have retired debt and built a solid financial plan. I have taken the hard steps to implement discipline in spending and investments. My family life is better than ever, and I have never loved so strong. I am more open with my wife about issues, and we hold more meaningful and purposeful conversations about where we have been, where we are, and where we aspire to be in five and ten years. Today, my life has more purpose. My belief system is solid, and I believe in myself first before choosing to believe in anything else. The reason is that outside entities can come and go; however, when we believe in ourselves, nothing can change it but us.

My mental and physical condition has improved, and it is the one area where I still need to work very hard to maintain sound footing. I wake up with purpose, and I am grateful for my life experiences—all of them. I no longer parse them out into good and bad experiences. There are only experiences, and we learn and grow from each one.

In my work, I returned to the leadership traits and principles learned in the Marine Corps and on my leadership journey. Relationships improved, influence was restored, and I returned to the leader I knew I could be in any situation: competent, confident, and getting things done the right way.

CHAPTER SUMMARY

1. Selfishness and poor personal accountability are the roots of poor self-leadership.
2. Allow yourself to have an honest conversation with yourself. It can serve as the first step to improve you.
3. Improvement starts with self-talk and an honest conversation with self. Without self-talk and an honest reconciliation of where you need to improve, you may never ask for help or help ourselves.
4. Each assignment, position, or opportunity may require a higher degree of self-leadership.

CALL TO ACTION

Now it is time that I gift you some work. That is right, no easy read; everyone is working. Sit for an hour, reflect on your life, and complete the following exercise. Important note: do not beat yourself up before, during, or after the activity below. Beating yourself up is not the objective. The objective is an honest and straightforward itemization, inventory, and understanding of why you got the exercise result.

1. Itemize the areas in your life where you are currently suffering from selfishness and poor personal accountability. Do not worry about being perfect. This is a brainstorming exercise, and in the following chapters, you will learn about key self-leadership assessment areas and criteria.

2. Determine what caused you to feel/act selfishly or lack personal responsibility.
   a. Did you put your comfort over others?
   b. Did you fail to take ownership of a shortfall or failure?

3. Start an internal conversation with the following priming questions:
   a. What is happening? (Requires total honesty)
   b. Why is it happening? (Primary actions or decisions that caused the issue)

c. How did it happen? (Personal actions or decisions that caused the issue)
d. What do I need to do to improve?
e. What resources do I need to improve?
f. What do I need to start doing?
g. What do I need to stop doing?
h. What do I need to keep doing?

CHAPTER 2

THE FOUNDATION OF PERSONAL RESPONSIBILITY PART ONE

The foundation of personal responsibility starts with a framework of leadership traits. Leadership traits are those distinguishing qualities that belong to a person or leader. Learning about and adopting traits happens in many ways. People acquire traits from their family/culture at home, organizational culture, and some selected leadership traits taught by organizations. In addition, people learn to emulate their parent's or caretakers' traits.

I have created a list of sixteen attributes that every leader must cultivate to achieve their highest potential. I will use this chapter to discuss the first half of the list and address the second half in the next chapter. The list represents a list of leadership traits at the root of Marine Corps life. Marines are expected to live and constantly cultivate these traits for their service tenure. Likewise, I have added a couple of attributes I picked up along my leadership journey. I cannot speak for every Marine who went before me or after my honorable discharge—I only know I have stayed very close to these my whole life. You may be surprised to know that these traits stick like glue if cultivated. We will discuss the leadership traits and provide a contextual anecdote for each one. Like success, leadership traits leave clues.

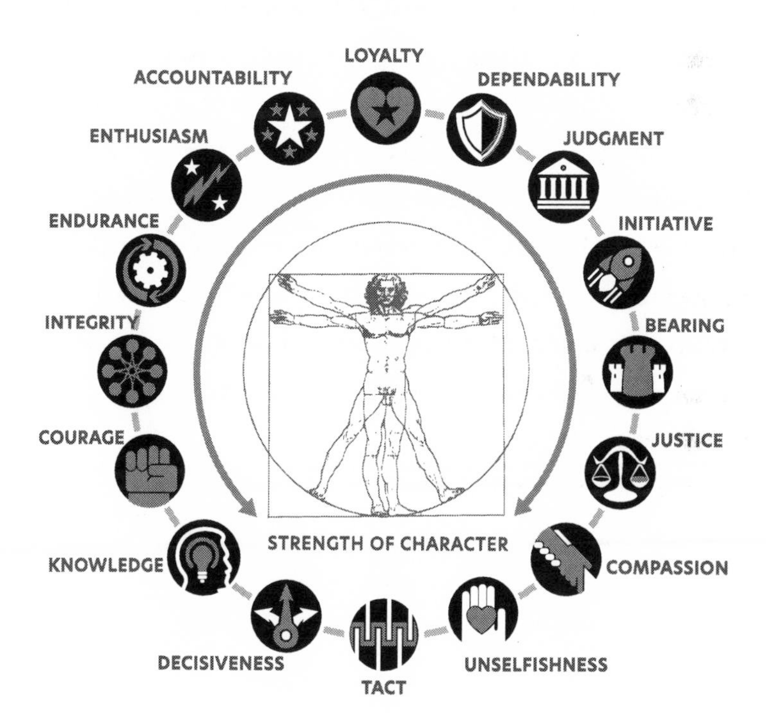

Eight Essential Leadership Traits

1. Justice

Giving reward and punishment according to the merits of the case in question. The ability to administer a system of rewards and punishments impartially and consistently.

Doesn't everyone receive equal justice? No, not close. Dictionaries define justice as moral rightness, righteousness, equitableness—what? That is hard to understand. Where is the measuring stick for moral rightness, righteousness, and equitableness? People do not understand this type of ambiguity. People do not know what it means and often confuse justice with the laws or rules.

The Marine Corps asks us to weigh facts and evidence, as the word *merit* would infer. Justice is not black and white like the rule of law. The challenge lies in impartially and consistently administering justice, which takes experience—that means making mistakes, but that is how you gain the experience necessary to do it well.

Look at the most mature systems and judges; they sometimes get justice wrong. As a person, you also administer self-justice. When you overstep your boundaries while speaking to a supervisor or loved one, you feel compelled to apologize. An apology is a justice based on the facts and evidence of why you put your foot in your mouth.

Justice works both ways, as inferred in the definition "giving reward and punishment." The reward is as important as the punishment. Arguably, the reward is more powerful than the punishment. In the context of reward, justice assures we award the accolades to the right person or group. You will always be sought out for guidance if you are known as the person who administers justice in a balanced manner. When folks seek your counsel, opportunities present themselves. Let's wrap up justice in simple terms. Justice is the ability to weigh facts and evidence unbiased with evenness.

2. Judgment

The ability to weigh facts and possible solutions on which to base sound decisions.

I always like talking about this one because it is interesting how people learn judgment. Personally, in my house growing up, judgment was swift and fair. I can remember my preteen years standing in front of my mom and her stating very bluntly while holding the fly swatter, "You better tell me the truth." In reflection, she was only trying to get the facts to weigh them so she could administer judgment and justice. I often escaped unscathed, although sometimes I received the wire end of the flyswatter—ouch. I want to believe she weighed the facts and evidence, yet, she had a switch, and if an eyebrow was cocked—game over, ha-ha.

Therefore, that is how I administered judgment for years until life taught me that, in some situations, we must pause to understand the problem before judging entirely. Some issues are so complex that it takes time to formulate an approach to a fair judgment.

Dictionaries define judgment as a decision or opinion after thorough deliberation. It makes sense, although somewhat generic. The Marine Corps defines judgment as "weighing facts and possible solutions on which to base sound decisions." Notice the slight nuance of "possible solutions." In this case, the Marine Corps emphasizes possible solutions to drive improvisation through judgment. A person carrying the potential solution additive improves our self-leadership by unlocking expanded thought when passing judgment.

The judgment trait definition ends with "sound decisions." Indeed, sound decisions are essential. You may ask, *why?* The reason is that the decision-making habits early in life form the foundation of our future decision-making. The Marine Corps recognizes this phenomenon and teaches sound decision-making from the get-go. Good decisions contribute to accomplishing the mission and build confidence in the individual. Make a wrong decision in the Marine Corps, and you will find out quickly. And that is great; feedback is the only way we improve and grow in any endeavor. We learn that even in making a wrong decision; so, do not get poopy pants if you receive feedback. The idea is not to make an egregious or fatal decision. Let's wrap up judgment in simple terms. Judgment uses facts while seeking innovative solutions to arrive at a good decision.

3. Dependability

The certainty of the proper performance of duty.

Dependability is one of the most important traits we can possess and maintain. Let's scrutinize "certainty of proper performance." The keyword is *certainty*. How can we build certainty of proper performance? Show up every day, do your job, learn your job, and when others need you or count on you—you must come through no matter what. And let me add that when you do not show up or you make excuses, people do not forget. They may say, "Oh, that is okay," or "I understand." Bullshit! You have demonstrated you are not dependable. Again, a trait like dependability builds confidence in the individual. More importantly, being known for dependability garners trust from others.

How about proper performance of duty? One might ask, *How do I know what is proper during my performance?* That is easy: we should always perform to a standard. Your standard regarding dependability is to show up every time, on time, and give your best. Sure, you might fall short or flop. Falling short is no shame, and if you try enough, you will flop. Get over it. At your work, you should know the performance standards. Make sure you are dependable and meet or exceed the standard.

I transferred to a different high school when I was a freshman because my school had ended the football program. Because the new school was in another district, I was ineligible to play during my freshman year. However, I never missed a practice, and I helped the team in any way I could. I loved to practice! I was dependable and recognized with the team's hardest worker award that year. I did not expect anything; I was new and just worked hard. It was a powerful lesson. Be dependable and work hard—opportunities will come. The next year, I had playing time on the varsity squad when the opportunity arose. Let's wrap up dependability in a simple way. You need to be there for yourself, and when others depend on you, make sure you show up.

4. Integrity

Uprightness of character and soundness of moral principles; includes the qualities of truthfulness and honesty.

Integrity is one of the most talked-about subjects in leadership. I have heard integrity called the currency of leadership. I would agree. But what exactly is integrity? Dictionaries define integrity as being honest and having strong moral principles. The Marine Corps shares the common theme of moral tenets and includes truthfulness and honesty.

Another explanation is the state of being whole and undivided. I like that one. I will tell you why. Integrity is closely related to sovereignty which we cover later in the discussion. Find a sovereign person, and you will find integrity and vice versa. One cannot exist without the other. Integrity is, without a doubt, the most tested trait of a person and leader.

Integrity, like the truth, has a personal and social cost. When you have integrity, you will lose friends and opportunities, and your circle will get smaller. People naturally want others to agree with them. Folks who maintain a good sense of integrity stand apart from the crowd. Sounds terrible, right? Not really.

The friends who stay are the ones you want. Do not worry; the opportunities you get are meaningful and without the burden of doing the wrong thing. When you practice integrity, your circle is purposely small.

The people I know with the highest integrity are uncompromising in most things they do. Like having blinders on with no second thoughts—they have conviction. From a self-leadership perspective, it is challenging to fool oneself regarding integrity. For example, do you skip a repetition if you are working out? Sure, missing a rep is a slight digression, but it may be a signal to examine other areas in your personal life where you may fall short of complete integrity. Guess what? Again, you will not be perfect at integrity.

The idea is to do your best and place integrity in the critical areas of your personal life. Let's wrap up integrity in a simple way. Let's wrap integrity up in a simple way. Integrity is doing the right thing when no one is looking. That means at the honor bar too!

5. Decisiveness

Ability to make decisions promptly and to announce them in a clear, forceful manner.

You know decisiveness when you hear it or see it in action. Decisiveness is accompanied by confidence and experience. We learn decision-making through experience; therefore, we learn how to be decisive.

Watch an American football game, and you will get a mental and physical demonstration of decisiveness. Pass-happy teams usually carry a quarterback with good decision-making abilities based on his experience. For example, Tom Brady has played professional football for twenty-one years. Brady knows the playbook like the back of his hand and has thousands of in-game repetitions. Therefore, decision-making and decisiveness are top traits for the quarterback.

Some would argue that sports, while unpredictable are predictable. For the most part, in football, the intent is unpredictable, and the basics of the sport are pretty predictable. He only has a few seconds to decide, yet that is plenty of time for him because of his experience. Simple, not so simple.

Tom Brady had to work exhaustively at decision-making at the professional level. Indeed, he learned quickly, yet he put in the work. Film study, opponent tendencies, knowing where his players should be and trusting them to be there, latitude to change the play, and the confidence to execute the play all weave into his experience at decisiveness. Seven Superbowl titles; yes, Tom Brady is a great decision maker.

For us laypeople, we must go through the same process. We must gain meaningful experience in some fields before making good decisions. Likewise, we may have more challenges than the Superbowl quarterback. By and large, we start our careers with very little training or experience. Most of us are quiet in our early careers, as we have no experience to lean on, so we are not announcing any prompt decisions and certainly not in a forceful manner.

We need the repetitions and expertise to cultivate decisiveness. When we wrestle with decisions, it more than likely reaches back to our experience—a depth of knowledge in the subject matter. On a personal level, the same concept applies. We make decisions based on repetitions in a particular situation. The more you experience an individual situation, the better you are at decision-making in that area (or should be). Let's wrap up decisive in simple terms. Decisive means using your experience to make decisions promptly and with confidence.

6. Tact

The ability to deal with others without creating offense.

Tact is a sure way to get noticed and an indicator of self-control. However, good tact does not mean one cannot directly address others. In direct types of communication, the intent and delivery matter. Most folks can take direct communication well if they know the purpose is to help the situation. Candid conversation eliminates beating around the bush and clarifies information to the receiving party. When both parties listen intently, direct communication swiftly moves the conversation. Moreover, it provides for shorter conversations. Note that building rapport sets the foundation for direct discussions.

One must always have the impression that others are sensitive. Stated another way, respect people's outlooks, viewpoints, and cultures. Demonstrating tact is a critical part of leading yourself effectively. The dividends are high for those who develop and cultivate tact in all situations. It takes practice, and the challenge is to maintain tact when subjects elicit an emotion or, worse, an emotional response. You will never be sorry for maintaining diplomacy. Think about it; you can never walk back a comment stated out of emotion that offends someone.

Poor tact can lead to a loss of trust. Conversely, you will never be sorry when you maintain tact, as you lost nothing and gained an opportunity to practice self-control. The dichotomy of tact is that everyone has a patience boundary. For some, the limitation is far-reaching, and for others, not so far.

Even when we have a cut-the-crap moment with someone, there is a way to deliver that too. Always state your position to allow the other party to save face. The relaxed and calm person usually wins the day in more than one way. They not only sound clear and articulate versus emotional and hijacked, but they gain respect.

I remember back in my Marine Corps days thinking tact is an art. It is one of those traits that some folks just have a knack for. In others, it is a journey and a constant learning process. I remember one colonel who had the best tact I ever witnessed.

He interfaced with folks at every grade flawlessly and not just in a glad-handing manner.

Tact is easy when it is easy. The challenge is when things are going badly, people are tired, frustrations mount, and you can cut the tension in the air with a knife. It is in these times that we need tact. I have seen it go both ways. A high demonstration of tact diffuses the situation and gets folks at ease in one conversation. Conversely, poor tact kills the mood, and folks take defensive positions.

Let's wrap up tact in a simple way. Tact shows respect and treats people how they like to be treated.

7. Initiative

Taking action in the absence of orders.

Boom! Act. Leadership, at its core, is action. Personal circumstances, work, and life often present us with ambiguous situations. Taking personal initiative and acting is a sure way to grow and learn.

Usually, high initiative leads inexperienced people to failure. I do not know how often I heard "recruit, good initiative, poor judgment in Marine boot camp." At first, I did not understand—I was taking the initiative. The lesson here is that there can be no effective initiative without thought or experience. The personal initiative must be intentional. Meaningful intent takes thought, and thought requires experience. Thought—not overthinking.

We are at trait number seven. Are you picking up a common thread in these traits? Experience, failure, and cultivation are common elements of leading yourself. Indeed, come to terms with this formula. The road is long. Better yet, self-leadership is a ride with no destination. We are a constant work in progress—back to discussing initiative. It is essential to take the initiative when in doubt. The absolute worst thing to do is stand still. Do not wait for some signal to come from your brain after overthinking the situation. Overthinking is not constructive and is limiting. Taking high initiative is sure to set you apart.

I would go on to say that high initiative is a performance differentiator. In performance, differentiation is the key to success. Everything is competitive, and high initiative will make a difference. I have seen initiative mistaken for showboating or trying to get brownie points. Likely, the people making these judgments wait to act and need instructions on what to do. Do not subscribe to that twisted idea of self-preservation. Instead, take the initiative and fail rather than depend on a higher authority to provide all the direction.

Taking high initiative requires some element of innate drive in a person. Similarly, people gain initiative when they learn that reward comes with acting. Most folks who have high initiative have that internal drive. Let's wrap up initiative in a simple way. Initiative is taking action to do something without being asked.

8. Enthusiasm

The display of sincere interest and exuberance in the performance of duty.

Enthusiasm is the most contagious leadership trait. Certain people light up a room with their genuine enthusiasm. When we find enthusiasm, we find passion. Ordinary men and women do extraordinary things when filled with enthusiasm. Enthusiasm and exuberance, as mentioned before, are infectious, and sometimes it just takes a spark to energize an entire team.

Unlike most other leadership traits, enthusiasm is a trait one can quickly demonstrate with few repetitions required to develop the attribute. The enthusiasm leadership trait intends to bring energy to yourself and the team. Marines do hard things; in life, we must do hard things. We might as well do them with enthusiasm.

When you can execute tasks that suck with exuberance, you have won and can embrace the suck. On the other hand, people have natural enthusiasm when they love what they do. One sure way to demonstrate enthusiasm is to speak with confidence. Your words say a lot. When you speak, you reveal who you are. Speak with energy and enthusiasm. Speaking with enthusiasm sets an example for others to follow.

Conversely, low energy works the other way and deflates you and those around you. Executing a task without enthusiasm may send a message that you are not interested or that the assignment is not essential.

In the execution of a job, low enthusiasm is a dangerous area. Consistently execute a task or assignment with some level of eagerness. Work to understand the task, assignment, or mission. Understanding builds a basis for enthusiasm.

Let's wrap up enthusiasm in a simple way. No matter the circumstance, good or bad, execute what you are doing in a manner consistent with a positive mindset and outward passion.

We have discussed the first eight leadership traits that build our character and competence. They are critical to self-leadership and the development of leadership character. Leadership traits, when cultivated, are performance differentiators. People who take the time to develop these leadership traits stand out from the crowd and make themselves available for opportunities. Likewise, these traits form the backbone of self-leadership.

CHAPTER SUMMARY

1. Justice and judgment require an impartial perspective and careful consideration of facts and evidence. People respect those who use justice and judgment impartially.
2. Dependability and integrity build trust with others. People seek to associate with those who build trust.
3. Decisiveness and tact support decision-making and communicating with others in the right way.
4. Initiative and enthusiasm display a proactive approach to the execution of tasks and are infectious to others.

CALL TO ACTION

1. Consider each of the following leadership traits: justice, judgment, dependability, integrity, decisiveness, tact, initiative, and enthusiasm. In a journal, write down your perception of each trait.

2. Try to identify where you might have learned each of these traits—at home, at school, at work, or somewhere else—and how you might improve or implement them in your daily life.

3. Identify people who exemplify each of these traits. If you are able, seek their guidance on developing those specific traits within yourself.

4. As you endeavor to cultivate these traits within yourself, journal about your progress and your evolving perception of each one. Compare this journal entry to your entry from Step 1 and note any changes.

CHAPTER 3

THE FOUNDATION OF PERSONAL RESPONSIBILITY PART TWO

Leadership traits are the foundation of self-leadership and personal responsibility. Without some structure and traits we can cultivate, we are flying blind. Worse yet, we may be succumbing to the status quo of doing what everyone else is doing just for the sake of doing it. It is imperative that we develop traits based on an embraced framework.

Now that you have mastered the first eight attributes that form the foundation of effective self-leadership, let's tackle the second half of that list.

Eight More Essential Leadership Traits

1. Bearing

Creating a favorable impression in carriage, appearance, and personal conduct at all times.

Good bearing speaks for itself. In challenging circumstances, maintaining your bearing may pave the way to an amicable solution. In a business setting, most people gravitate to the cool and calm person in all situations. For example, if you have ever experienced mediation, the mediator always has a suitable bearing. The last thing we need at mediation is an emotional mediator to stoke the fires.

Bearing is highly dependent on reactions to emotions. Find a person who gets emotional, and you will observe suspect bearing. Conversely, a person who possesses good bearing usually has strong self-control. In regard to bearing, control in any situation is the main idea.

Poor bearing does not make you a bad person. You might lose it from time to time, but the key phrase in the definition is "at all times." Herein lies the challenge. Life happens, and emotions come into play. We get hijacked. Good bearing comes with time, maturity, and perspective.

Over time, we learn that certain things are not worth a reaction, response, or emotional investment. Some things do not matter, like the person who likes to push buttons. Just give them the silent treatment or some emphatic murmuring, like *uh-huh*, *I understand*, or *yeah*. I promise they will stop and move on to the next victim.

Creating a favorable impression is usually the first thing people notice—hence, the old adage of "first impressions." Indeed, making an excellent first impression is essential and easy. Dress the part, stand straight and confident, and announce yourself in a straightforward and friendly manner; there is nothing complicated about it.

The key to getting known for a good impression is dressing the part, but the world has changed, and people dress differently across various cultures. It is tough to nail down how one should dress and what comprises a good appearance. Moreover, we have personal and work dress codes. Learn what is acceptable and what is not. Again, perspectives have changed. Appearance includes hair, body odor, nails, and the like. Sorry, it is true, and it matters. Check yourself. Folks can choose to maintain a clean body or be unkempt. It is a personal choice; however, we must keep some standard of self-care. Look good, feel good, do good. Let's wrap up bearing in a simple way. Show up looking presentable for the occasion and stay in control of your emotions.

2. Unselfishness

Avoidance of providing for one's own comfort and personal advancement at the expense of others.

Bingo! The most critical leadership trait probably deserves a book of its own. It is hard to know where to start with this trait. There are many options, so I will start simple.

First, let's talk about something we can relate to. How often have you seen someone place their comfort or welfare in front of others? You may see it three to four times per day or more if you work in a large organization. Some folks try to hide it by intellectualizing the situation. "I am not able to help on that because I have higher priorities," only to find them Facebooking or some other ass-grabbing extracurricular activity.

Meanwhile, the team suffers from this simple form of selfishness. On the other hand, some good souls move heaven and earth to support anything they can so everyone benefits by delivering the business plan or mission. These are the people you want next to you.

There are many ways to view unselfishness. Making a conscious effort to serve others is unselfish and fulfilling. Always putting others first develops the trait of unselfishness, but it does not mean you put others first to your detriment. On the contrary, you must take care of yourself. Just like putting your oxygen mask on first on a plane, the same applies to unselfishness.

From time to time, out of love or some other internal driver, we will ignore that rule and sacrifice ourselves for others. This perspective on unselfishness has deep meaning. Marines and soldiers have jumped on grenades to save others in the military.

SEAL team member Michael Murphy knowingly sacrificed his life for his team during Operation Red Wings. How about a mom who protects her children from an abusive husband knowing she cannot overpower her abuser? These examples are the ultimate demonstration of unselfishness. The ultimate sacrifice.

How do these courageous people decide to make the sacrifice? They are people who live their values with solid conviction and have the will to protect and accomplish the mission at any cost. They have made peace with the notion of zero-sum outcomes. If these brave souls can sacrifice their lives for a just cause, how can we not get past petty selfishness? Please think about this and then look in the mirror.

On a personal level, how many times do we make selfish choices? Remember, we are selfish in actions and words. Being selfish is the absolute worst trait, yet we do it all the time. When I learned to become genuinely unselfish, it was a new perspective.

For example, I started trying to win the relationship instead of winning the conversation. Most of my relationships improved from this simple approach. Get over yourself, and save yourself from being hijacked and the like.

No one said anything about self-leadership being easy. It is not easy, and it takes constant work. But what if putting in some hard work on selfishness improves other areas of your life? I promise that different parts of your life will improve exponentially.

Changes in behavior change a person's perspective, and it is perspective that causes the shifts in your mind. In a sense, you must be willing to be someone new. For some, this is a challenge; it was a challenge for me. *What will people think? How will they react to my new approach? Will they think it is fake?* People will thank you for changing for the better. Those thoughts are natural and scary, but always remember that improvement is the other side of doubt and fear. Let's wrap up unselfishness in simple terms. Put others before yourself and your comforts.

3. Courage

The mental quality that recognizes fear of danger or criticism but enables one to proceed in the face of it with calmness and firmness.

The first thought I always have when courage presents itself is the quote by Teddy Roosevelt in his speech upon leaving office in 1910:

> It is not the critic who counts; not the man who points out how the strong man stumbles or where the doer of deeds could have done them better. The credit belongs to the man who is actually in the arena, whose face is marred by dust and sweat and blood; who strives valiantly; who errs, who comes short again and again because there is no effort without error and shortcoming; but who does actually strive to do the deeds; who knows great enthusiasms,

> the great devotions; who spends himself in a worthy cause; who at best knows, in the end, the triumph of high achievement, and who at the worst, if he fails, at least fails while daring greatly, so that his place shall never be with those cold and timid souls who neither know victory nor defeat.

It is hard to say it better than Roosevelt. Indeed, to possess courage is to dare greatly.

Although some men are born to fight, they still require courage in their lives to keep going toward the gunfire. Courage is stepping into the arena even when we know there is peril, and we might come out on the short end. If success is on the other side of fear, courage gets us past the fear.

When I was young, the military and football represented courage. My dad was in World War II, Korea, and Vietnam (three times). We never talked much about it; however, he would tell me where he was and some details of what it was like serving. As I grew older and learned about the military and the wars, I had a new respect for his sacrifice and courage. My dad was always calm, and few things could get him worked up.

Not all my heroes wear capes. When people imagine courage, most people might think of a Spartan Warrior, a soldier, or someone playing a contact sport. While each must have some element of courage, believing these types of people are the only ones who have courage is a result of pop culture and movies. However, I met a woman in a book workshop I attended who demonstrated as much, if not more, courage than I have personally witnessed. As far as this book goes, her name is "LS."

We participated in multiple modules on book writing during the workshop, and one module was, who are you writing this book for? When it was LS's turn, she was stoic and silent for what felt like a couple of minutes. Everyone felt tension build in the room. When LS spoke, her voice shook, and she paused multiple times. Finally, she divulged that she was writing her book for parents who lost a child, as she lost her son and found out while at work. She faced fear in a roomful of strangers, and her courage was extraordinary. It was a raw human moment, a rare occurrence, and something I will never forget. LS is a small woman by stature, yet her heart is as big as a pumpkin—her courage even more enormous. Although we do not know one another well, LS has become one of my heroes. I know she is going to write a great book.

What gets in the way of courage? Many things. Mostly, we have anxiety about what others will think of us. We fear judgment. What about our insecurities? I believe folks struggle with both. Also, self-doubt is a killer of courage. However, there is a solution to insecurity and fear of judgment. Preparation and knowledge provide the footing for courage. Learn your trade, business, and job, and stay consistent and disciplined; then you will find that you will choose situations with increasing difficulty where courage is necessary. It is a natural evolution.

Humans are naturally predisposed to compete—survival in the most primal form. Even introverts are competitive. We may not see it, but they are thinking about it. I have seen introverts display some of the most profound courage. The aggressive type A or Alpha do not have a monopoly on courage. In my experience, there are no alphas, no betas, just people. Push a person far enough, and you will see courage come out.

Some might say it is fight or flight; I challenge that notion—some folks are quiet. After all, most folks who proclaim Alpha status may not even know what Alpha means. What is an Alpha? In nature, the Alpha is the individual animal at the apex of the tribe. With seven billion people roaming the earth, I believe that definition is difficult to apply to humans. It is possible to set criteria and rate people in seriatim (top to bottom) in any group, but does that define the Alpha? I am sure there are too many opinions on what Alpha means to people, so let's leave it there. In simple terms, courage is going out into the arena knowing you might lose but having the confidence to try despite fear and danger.

4. Knowledge

Understanding of a science or an art. The range of one's information, including professional knowledge and an understanding of your Marines/people.

Webster's defines knowledge as information, understanding, or skill you get from experience and education. I believe Webster's is right and tracks with the Marine Corps definition. The Marine Corps asked us to include an understanding of our Marines. Likewise, as civilians, we must understand others.

This book focuses on self-leadership, and the Marine Corps approaches the definition of knowledge from a people-leadership perspective. The smallest unit is a fire team in the Marine combat arms (infantry and combat engineers). There is one fire team leader and three support Marines. A Marine may have to step up to lead others in a heartbeat, so everything is about readiness and leading, hence, the inclusion of understanding your Marines.

Likewise, we should appreciate the people we lead. What does that mean? Simple. Every person is unique. We all come from different backgrounds, cultures, and experiences. Knowing your people requires some depth in diversity. Knowing your people makes you a better leader. Take time to learn about people. Research their interests, culture, and customs, as it helps to find common ground.

You will find that respect is a close cousin to knowledge. Having more knowledge on a subject means having more information. Once we are informed, we can have a higher capacity to give respect to someone's interests, culture, and customs.

People approach learning knowledge in different ways as well. First, you should know what type of learning best suits you. For example, some are visual learners, and others prefer to read copious amounts of book material. Another way to learn is by doing the work or task. Hit the high points of the subject matter and start doing. Finally, our natural curiosity makes us ask questions, so we continually build on our knowledge.

Let's explore the term *range of information*. I like this subtlety; it makes me think of tactical (how), strategic (what), and operational knowledge of the subject matter.

As new employees, we usually learn the tactical stuff first—how things get done. For example, let's take business planning; the strategic part is what the business plan sets out to accomplish. Higher returns through differentiated operational performance. The tactics in this situation would be the more minor, task-oriented activities such as, let's say, focused sales in a particular region.

In the military, the mission articulates the strategy (e.g., push back threats south of the area of operations at a specific coordinate). The tactics are the way the supporting units execute the plan (e.g., recon, patrols, and attacking the main force of an enemy to push them back). Operational knowledge comes once we understand how strategy and tactics work together.

I can remember a few aha moments in my work when I got to a point where I understood the strategy and tactics behind what I was doing. It opened a new dimension and a different way to think about the subject matter. Knowledge is like leadership; it takes constant effort to learn information, understand, and develop skills. Knowledge is a journey, and we are always between the bookends of beginner and mastery. Let's wrap up knowledge in a simple way. Knowledge is the cumulative amount of information and understanding you possess in a particular area.

5. Loyalty

The quality of faithfulness to country, the Navy, the unit, to one's seniors, subordinates, and peers. (For the purposes of this book, we exclude the Navy if you are a civilian/not in the Navy or Marine Corps.)

Loyalty is a trait that all people look for in others. Prospective employers and significant others are always on the lookout for loyal people. People and businesses covet faithful people because they are predictable. As the definition infers, peers seek loyalty too.

What about loyalty to self? How can we be loyal to others if we are not first loyal to ourselves? When we break promises to ourselves, it damages other parts of our leadership framework.

The absence of loyalty adversely impacts dependability because the two traits interweave. Dependability is similar, although our definitions offer distinction—certain performances of duty and faithfulness—both infer a commitment. The key to loyalty is commitment. In all honesty, loyalty comes from the heart. The person has a desire to be loyal, which fulfills some want in the individual.

Loyalty between peers is essential, as it is the essence of teamwork. Find a team with high loyalty to one another, and you will find an effective team. In a team, loyalty is a 360 attribute—meaning that the individual is loyal to peers, subordinates, and seniors. Loyalty, in this way, creates a high-trust environment. In a highly effective team, all members must demonstrate loyalty. Trust and connection to individuals build loyalty.

How about loyalty to self? Like trust and belief, if a person is not loyal to themselves, they will struggle to be devoted to others; this is a critical area where people misunderstand the importance of leading themselves. Find someone who is self-destructive, a bad decision maker, or shortsighted; most likely, they cannot sustain loyalty to others.

I served the last two and a half years of my tour in the Marine Corps with a good buddy from Cairo, Georgia. I still feel a connection to him to this day. Unfortunately, we have drifted apart over the decades; however, I spoke to him last year, and it was like we never left one another's side.

Similarly, in 2003 while watching the evening news, I saw a picture of one of my buddies who died in Iraq. He was the fifty-second American killed in the GWOT. I immediately froze in my living room, dropped my book, put my head down, and cried. I still felt a deep sense of loyalty to him. He was a sweet guy, sharp in all ways, and he never raised his voice. Also, he was small in stature but tough as they come.

When I look back on my time in the Marine Corps, I believe that it was the transformational change and suffering together that built trust and loyalty. Absent the suffering, there are things we can do to build genuine loyalty with people and our loved ones. Showing respect, vulnerability, and compassion to others consistently is a great start. Forgiving and letting go of grudges that erode relationships builds loyalty.

6. Endurance

Mental and physical stamina measured by the ability to withstand pain, fatigue, stress, and hardship.

The ability to endure is the absolute performance differentiator. When committed, a person who possesses endurance can achieve most anything imagined within the realm of reality, and sometimes more. How many times have we seen humans do superhuman stuff? Sure, a big heart (literally), big lungs, and healthy red blood cells help. For instance, African wild dogs naturally have big hearts and big lungs for their size. As a result, they can run full speed for two hours while chasing gazelles. The gazelle, while faster, will exhaust and eventually become dinner. Physically the same applies to humans. The difference is that the wild dog has adapted to survive.

On the other hand, humans might have a large heart, lungs,

and healthy red blood cells, yet they may have the drive of a snail. What is the point here? Willpower and psychology in humans drive individual physical and mental endurance.

When a person first decides and then commits, the mind can take the body further than previously imagined.

I remember one morning in Okinawa, we fell in for physical training (PT). Our company First Sargent was a fair hard-ass. The old breed, for sure. The First Sargent instructed us to return to barracks, change out our silky greens shorts and go fasters (sneakers) for our battle dress uniform (BDU), camo trousers, and boots, and grab a canteen. The order was simple and as ominous as the First Sergeant laid it down. The big green weenie was afoot, and I thought this was not good.

After returning to formation and cover and aligning, we immediately heard, "Your asses are mine." First Sargent was a runner, and we knew he could run forever, yet our PT runs were always of the nominal five-mile variety. However, that day our PT session and run would be different. I had run the mile and mile relay (fourth leg) in high school, which was the furthest I had ever run. So, running five miles, to me, was quite an accomplishment.

My lungs always burned after a couple of miles; I thought I had asthma and a five-mile limit, but there was something about being surrounded by your platoon mates that turned off the pain—it is hard to explain. Indeed, together everyone goes further. I would find out later in life during an overseas assignment physical that my lungs are undersized. Years later, after attending a personal development course, I found out I am slightly anemic. Slightly undersized lungs, somewhat anemic, but I never fucking quit. Although it did not always look good, I finished nonetheless.

That day in Okinawa, we ran fourteen miles in boots and trousers. When you have run five miles most every day for a couple of years, you do not need a finish line to know when you have reached the five-mile mark. Personally, the sixth mile was the most challenging for me. I had to work through a mental boundary.

That is the point about endurance. It is a huge mental obstacle when we go to the edge of where we have been in previous times. The dichotomy is at the edge; there is a huge adrenaline rush, fear, and excitement coupled with some self-doubt. Again, hard to define. Pushing through the mental and physical boundaries is something you will never forget. You will always be able to recall that special moment when you drive past pain, fatigue, stress, and hardship. Let's wrap up endurance in simple terms. Endurance is your ability to withstand and continue through mental and physical challenges.

7. Compassion

The ability to show consideration and understanding for the hardships of others and oneself.

While this point is not derived from the Marine Corps

specifically, arguably, compassion is the highest form of leadership. Compassion applies to self-leadership as well. How do we show self-compassion? Showing self-compassion is similar to the way we show others compassion. When we see others in agony, pain, strife, and hardships, we show kindness and understanding of their situation.

In the same way, we must be compassionate toward ourselves. Unfortunately, many individuals struggle with showing others compassion due to their upbringing. If people do not learn how to show compassion while growing up, they are most likely unable to practice showing kindness to others. Similarly, people have a hard time showing self-compassion. The absence of compassion can hurt relationships and oneself. Leading by example is the best way to show others how to have compassion.

People need to see genuine compassion at the right moment to understand. They may have a sense of compassion but be unable or unwilling to show compassion because of mental barriers caused by their mistreatment. As a result, people often treat others as they were in their past.

It is difficult—but not impossible—to instill the meaning of compassion in people who are otherwise incapable of showing compassion. First, it is essential to build the capacity to cope with anger and maintain self-regulation in people unable to extend compassion to themselves. It is like forgiveness—people who cannot forgive themselves struggle to forgive others genuinely.

Developing compassion for yourself is essential, and there are effective ways to do it. The first step is to look inward and silence your inner critic and the harsh judgment that accompanies this voice. Start with forgiving yourself for small things and mentally work up to forgiving yourself for larger issues where you assign self-blame. Embrace challenges instead of running from them. Live in the moment instead of the past and future to remove possible negative self-talk. Finally, express gratitude for what you have right now instead of dwelling on what you do not have. Let's wrap up compassion in simple terms. Compassion is the ability to show care and concern for yourself and others.

8. Accountability

The eagerness to accept responsibility for one's actions.

Like the point above, this attribute is one I have gleaned from civilian life and the Marine Corps. Personal accountability centers on your decisions and actions. Let's start with the first element: decisions. I love to correlate choices to forks in the road. Think about all the decisions you make in a day. We make hundreds of them. Some critical choices pit us against our traits and values. Moreover, we encounter moral and ethical dilemmas. These are the choices that define the way we lead ourselves.

When faced with a decision, we follow up with action, where the aforementioned leadership attributes pay dividends. Why, you ask? The answer is simple. We make good and bad decisions all the time. But with a solid commitment to our leadership traits, we will act in the right way no matter if we make good or bad decisions. Operating in the right way is personal accountability for our actions.

Failure and accountability are interlinked. When we fail, we must own our failures: every part of them. Owning our failures builds personal accountability. As we grow in our leadership journey and lead others, strong personal accountability eliminates blaming other organizations, teams, and outside influences for our shortcomings and failures. Accountability is like enthusiasm; it spreads quickly because people see others leading by example. Let's not overwork accountability and wrap it up in simple terms. Accountability is owning your actions after you have decided and acted. You own the results, good or bad. Let's wrap up accountability in a simple way. Accountability is proactively taking ownership of your actions.

Leadership Traits Fill the Space Between Decision and Action

There is a void between decision and action. It takes a microsecond to choose a behavior to match your action. For example, let's take the trait *bearing* and examine a scenario where you select a response. You are in a passionate discussion about the yearly budget, and finance attacks your justification. You know finance is playing the numbers game, but your estimates support minimum, regulatory compliance and corporate expectations. The accountant presses you and trivializes your competence. Yet, you are standing on the facts.

Cutting the budget means you have to cut back on staffing, and you will not meet performance expectations. Finally, after some back and forth, finance informs you that your budget is 40 percent lower than the year before with the exact same expectations. With all the weight of the cut budget, the finance manager then asks you if you can make it work.

Will you lose your bearing or keep calm and carry on? I am not saying you should not be upset, but will it help the situation if you lambaste the finance manager? It is in these situations when you must keep your bearing. By maintaining your bearing, you pass the moment of truth where you can decide to lose your temper or maintain emotional control. Your leadership training and experience bridge the gap between outcomes in stressful situations when you arm yourself with the emotional tools to make clear decisions under duress.

Tying It All Together

After reading all the traits and other supporting information, you probably ask yourself, *How do I connect the dots, and where do I start? How do I measure my progress against the standards in this chapter?* Not to worry; we have you covered. We can work on one leadership trait per week or try the grouping approach.

First, let's examine how we can do some incremental work here. So, the acronym is JJ DID TIE BUCKLE. Likewise, we have added CA. Each letter represents the first letter of the traits itemized in Chapters 2 and 3. The abbreviation has four groupings: perfect. Generally, there are four weeks in one month, so try tackling one group per week while always including compassion and accountability.

Alternatively, you can work on one trait per week or approximately three times in one year. You get the point; parse out the traits to match your appetite to improve. For those of you who are primarily desk workers, place an index card near the bottom of your monitor as a constant reminder to practice the traits. Others who work in the field may keep a copy in their pocket or their field kit. I can tell you it is a powerful reference and a good forcing function.

DEFINITIONS

LEADERSHIP is the sum of those qualities of intellect, human understanding, and moral character that enables a person to inspire and to control a group of people successfully.

LEADERSHIP TRAITS or characteristics are those qualities of personality which are of greatest assistance in obtaining confidence, respect, obedience and loyal cooperation.

LEADERSHIP PRINCIPLES are guides for the proper exercise of command.

LEADERSHIP TECHNIQUES are actions taken by the leader. A leadership technique should:

1. Be guided by the Leadership Principles.
2. Exhibit the good traits of the commander.
3. Be consistent with the situation.
4. Contribute toward accomplishing, or accomplish, one or both of the responsibilities of a commander.

COMBAT EFFICIENCY is the ability of the unit to accomplish an assigned mission in the shortest possible time with the minimum loss of life and waste of material.

LEADERSHIP PRINCIPLES

1. Be Technically and Tactically Proficient.
2. Know Yourself and Seek Self-Improvement.
3. Know Your Men and Look Out for Their Welfare.
4. Keep Your Men Informed.
5. Set the Example.
6. Insure that the Task is Understood, Supervised, and Accomplished.
7. Train Your Men as a Team.
8. Make Sound and Timely Decisions.
9. Develop a Sense of Responsibility Among Subordinates.
10. Employ Your Command in Accordance With Its Capabilities.
11. Seek Responsibility and Take Responsibility for Your Actions.

OBJECTIVES OF LEADERSHIP

Primary—Accomplishment of Mission.

Secondary—Welfare of the men.

INDICATIONS OF MILITARY LEADERSHIP

MORALE is the state of mind of the individual. This state of mind is dependent upon his attitudes toward everything that affects him.

DISCIPLINE is the prompt obedience to orders and in the absence of orders, the initiation of appropriate action.

ESPRIT DE CORPS is the loyalty to, pride in and enthusiasm for a unit shown by the members of that unit.

PROFICIENCY is the technical, tactical and physical ability to do a job well.

ESSENTIAL LEADERSHIP TRAITS

INTEGRITY.—Uprightness of character and soundness of moral principle, absolute truthfulness and honesty.

KNOWLEDGE.—Acquired information, including professional knowledge and an understanding of your men.

COURAGE.—A mental quality that recognizes fear of danger or criticism but enables a man to proceed in the face of it with calmness and firmness.

DECISIVENESS.—Ability to reach decisions promptly and to announce them in a clean, forceful manner.

DEPENDABILITY.—The certainty of the proper performance of duty.

INITIATIVE.—Seeing what has to be done and commencing a course of action, even in the absence of orders.

TACT.—The ability to deal with others without creating offense.

JUSTICE.—The quality of being impartial and consistent in exercising command.

ENTHUSIASM.—The display of sincere interest and exuberance in the performance of duty.

BEARING.—Creating a favorable impression in carriage, appearance, and personal conduct at all times.

ENDURANCE.—The mental and physical stamina measured by the ability to stand pain, fatigue, distress and hardship.

UNSELFISHNESS.—Avoidance of providing for ones comfort and personal advancement at the expense of others.

LOYALTY.—Faithfulness to country, Corps, and unit, and to your seniors and subordinates.

JUDGMENT.—The quality of weighing facts and possible solutions on which to base sound decisions.

Attributes shape a person's character and serve as the most critical component of the self-leadership framework. In turn, leadership traits require context, understanding, and cultivation.

CHAPTER SUMMARY

1. Bearing and unselfishness provide a template for keeping our emotions in check and putting others before our own comfort.
2. Courage and knowledge lay the groundwork to meet challenges head on when the odds are not in our favor and set the expectation to acquire depth in our areas of interest.
3. Loyalty and endurance stress the importance of devotion and the will to endure physical and mental hardships.
4. Compassion and accountability remind us of the want to alleviate others' distress and ground us in the mentality that in self-leadership the buck stops with us.

CALL TO ACTION

1. Consider each of the following leadership traits: bearing, unselfishness, courage, knowledge, loyalty, endurance, compassion, and accountability. In a journal, write down your perception of each trait.
2. Create a plan for improving each trait incrementally. Decide how often and when you will tackle each trait. Write notes or set reminders for yourself. Block out time in your schedule if necessary.
3. Identify people who exemplify each of these traits. If you can, seek their guidance on developing those specific traits within yourself.
4. As you endeavor to cultivate each trait within yourself, journal about your progress and your evolving perception of the traits in question.

CHAPTER 4

YOUR LEADERSHIP CHARACTER

Character, part and parcel of trust, is critical to developing your individual leadership character. It is the mental and moral code by which you govern or lead yourself. We demonstrate our character in many ways; it is how we navigate difficult situations.

Back in Chapters 2 and 3, we discussed leadership traits. Those traits and others build our leadership character. As an analogy, just like constructing a house, building strong leadership character requires robust materials. Our home becomes stronger the harder we work to develop leadership traits and practice values. An attribute or value that started as a sheet of tin becomes stone. Indeed, your leadership character builds over time. As the old cliché goes—Rome was not built in one day. Your leadership character is no exception. There are critical times in your life to make good choices related to your character. The younger we are, the more chances to make a wrong decision and the longer the recovery time.

"Character is Destiny."

—Heraclitus

As an individual, your values and work ethic build your character. In turn, your character forms the groundwork for your leadership character. Your leadership character forms by self-governance, cultivated values, trusting yourself, staying sovereign, and developing a reputation for doing your job well.

What Is Character?

Let's start this discussion by defining character. The Greeks first used the word *charaktēr*, which means *to scratch or engrave* in the Greek language. In antiquity, artists, inventors, and writers all had unique marks. Some were impressed and others stamped into the wax. Everyone knew their work by the distinctive marks and engravings of their symbols.

Along the way, the word character came to mean the sum of a person's qualities and the traits that make them distinct. In modern times, dictionaries define character as moral excellence, firmness, and features that make up and distinguish an individual.

There are many different contexts and perspectives on character. However, one view that we can all agree on is that character is who you are. How you treat others and self-govern yourself defines your individual leadership character. Treating others right is a sure sign of a person who has a strong leadership character. No one says you must like people; it is your right to have opinions and judgments. Likewise, you do not have to be liked by everyone. However, we must always treat people right, and we expect the same in return.

Treating people right means we treat them with dignity and respect. You may not respect others' behaviors and what they do, but you must respect them as a person. Sometimes this is hard—when it is hard, and you treat people with respect, you build your character.

In Chapter 9, we will discuss celebrating others' successes. Sometimes that is hard to do for various reasons, but it pays dividends. Genuinely treating others well works in the same way. Unfortunately, sometimes we treat others with less than acceptable respect as individuals. Resist this temptation with all the energy you can muster.

Self-governing is when you are not easily manipulated or controlled by outside forces. We will talk more about sovereignty in Chapter 8, but for now, you should know that self-governing is more than staying sovereign, although it does play a leading role. Governance is known as how people run an organization or entity. The same applies to self-governance. How you conduct yourself is the way you self-govern. Self-awareness, reflection, improvement, and balancing esteem are important parts of self-governance. These main elements provide a framework for the individuals' self-governance.

Individual Character versus Leadership Character

How are individual character and individual leadership character different? The two are close, but there is a difference. In your leadership character, you may possess and cultivate traits that allow you to lead others effectively; it is how people see you personally as a leader. The difference is that your leadership character must consider and include impacts on other people and stakeholders. Some differentiating elements of leadership character are people skills, strategic business skills, engagement, etc. As individuals, we adopt core values and traits that engrave our character with some cultivation.

Yet, when leading others, as an individual, we must demonstrate that we adhere to additional values. For example, we must lead others with a level of temperance. Likewise, we must show genuine care for others. There are other dimensions of leadership characteristics, such as communication style. Your communication style as a leader might be open, honest, and direct, while your interpersonal communication style is subtle. Leading by example is the most crucial component of your individual leadership character.

I developed my leadership character early in life by emulating my parents, sports coaches, martial arts teachers, and some military leaders. Developing leadership character is like forging, and it appears at different times for different people. By age twenty-three, I had been through twelve years of football, seven years of martial arts, and four years of the Marine Corps.

Moreover, my father was a veteran of World War II, Korea, and Vietnam with thirty-two years of service. My mother was 100 percent Serbian. I was forged in a certain way, and by the time I finished my tour in the Marine Corps, I had a unique character engraving. The die was cast.

Football taught me consistency, discipline, and hard work. I also learned about how great leaders treated groups of men. I want to believe that most of my football coaches had the right intentions, no matter their behavior. Some were direct, some acted like a guiding hand, and one was a total head case. My football coaches' approaches and personalities were an example of what I would experience throughout my life. Football also taught me about feedback and the intentions behind the input. Football is a sport of constant feedback.

Martial arts were the first place I learned about living and training to a code. In Tae Kwon Do, I realized the tenets of courtesy, integrity, perseverance, self-control, and indomitable spirit. Martial arts taught me about progression and the hard work it takes to achieve the next level. There are always new things to learn in martial arts, and we work toward higher levels of technique; there is little room for complacency. I did not achieve a black belt until I was thirty-seven.

Martial arts and the tenets of Tae Kwon Do etched my leadership character. My most outstanding martial arts achievement is teaching Tae Kwon Do, which has been a privilege. In my lower-belt youth classes, I learned about a big gap between those who could catch on and perform the kicks and strikes as intended and those who could not. I talked about this with one of the senior instructors, whose feedback was that each child does something well. That always stuck with me, and I have made that correlation to leading myself and others since then. Each person does something well. It is vital as a leader that your character recognizes and accepts people as they are and not how you want them to be—demonstrating that you are willing to acknowledge what people do well is a leadership character trait. Attempting to transform people into something they cannot achieve or focusing on their flaws is destructive and counterproductive to leadership character.

The Marine Corps forged my leadership character. The deepest parts of my leadership character come from my four-year tour. For four years of your committed tour of duty, the Corps expects you to live the traits and principles. Like a business demand, you are constantly kept in check by reminders from peers, superiors, and to some degree, subordinates. It is what makes the Marine Corps special and unique. One cannot leave the Corps without developing leadership character. Some mistakenly call this type of indoctrination brainwashing—on the contrary, Marines live to a code. When you live something, it becomes part of you. Stated more directly, Marines live, eat, breathe, and shit leadership.

I am fifty-two, and along the way I have always allowed myself and challenged myself to grow and strengthen my character. It served me well until I reached the higher echelons of the corporate world. In some corporate cultures, money matters more than people. This is a fact and may be hard for some to hear. Some will deny it until their face turns blue. These are the people who see others as servants rather than humans. I could never buy into that mode of thinking. I preferred to serve others.

We Do Not Talk About and Measure Character Enough

I found that character is the least talked-about part of promotions, recruiting, and leader development. Some large corporations have a myopic view of leadership and often value skills over character.

It is not to say that large corporations do not have leaders with strong character—just that it is not a focus area.

Often people with mastery skills are forgiven for their poor character. Even promoted despite flawed character. This practice is an affront to those who work hard to demonstrate strong character. For some reason, corporations and business cultures have an aversion to talking about and measuring people's character. I believe they are afraid that folks may perceive it as questioning someone's character when critiquing it.

I believe grading character is achievable, but it matters how we deliver the feedback to the individual. Feedback given with the intent to improve might be hard to hear, but the individual is more likely to accept the feedback. Likewise, feedback about someone's character delivered with negative intent is a relationship killer. Discussing character is dicey at best; however, it is essential for growth.

How do we cultivate and form individual leadership character? A framework of values and traits, experience, and meaningful repetition creates your leadership character. On the other hand, you might develop leadership character without a framework. Some folks do not know about traits and values because they have not had leadership training. We train athletes and people how to acquire and develop technical skills, so why not make leadership character training compulsory for every organization? People without leadership training may not have a well-intentioned leadership character. This is because they have allowed each experience to shape them without boundaries. In contrast, a person with a framework of values and traits grows within the confines of a chosen framework and develops a unique leadership character.

Strong Character Differentiates Performance

Individual leadership character is a differentiator. You need to develop a unique leadership character. Each person is special; your leadership character develops in the same way. Character development is a continuum. So, how does leadership character serve as a differentiator? Your leadership character makes you a good fit for specific leadership opportunities. No leader is good at leading across all fields of leadership. Leadership is always a balance of building trust, using influence effectively, and using authority as a mechanism to get things done.

The latter is a last resort, yet authority used in the right way to get things done is a valid leadership approach. Some leadership assignments require open, honest, and direct communication. Others require a softer approach. Some require mastery of organizational skills, whereas others require less organizational skills but more people-development focus. I hope you are starting to get the point here.

When appointed to a leadership role that does not fit your leadership character, do not be surprised if you fail. The organization did not set you up for success or adequately evaluate you. However, do not lament your failure too long; keep moving and find a better fit.

You are not an island either. The strongest leaders require a support structure. I have seen many leaders fail because those around them could not do their jobs.

After applying for a management consulting job at my old company, I was the slate's successful candidate. Supposedly, the job was a project scenario with a team of disciplines across the business. True enough, the team included disciplines from HR to operations. However, each team member reported to others in their discipline. Therefore, the assignment was 100 percent influential. My style is open, honest, and direct, and I ask people to work. Unfortunately, my style immediately clashed with some members of the team. My straightforward communication style was not the right fit for this job.

Character Is More Important than Ability

Personal character is more important than skills. Skills are easy to acquire, and character takes hard work and consistency. Have you ever known a person who is not very skilled but seems to get things done? They are likely surviving and thriving on their character. For them, that is enough, and they probably add some cohesion to the team.

They are the person who is good at mending others' fences for them, who sacrifices their ego for the betterment of the team, and who seems to make everyone around them better. They can temper an aggressive personality and motivate the passive personalities. This type of person is always working on their personal character, focusing on *who* they are instead of *what* they are. These people brim with confidence. They do not take sides; they provide only their perspective. And they are usually the hardest workers and most reliable when called on. I will take someone like this over a highly skilled and low-character individual ten out of ten times.

None of Us Have a Perfect Character

If you find someone who claims to have perfect character, be suspicious. In all honesty, it is hard to have imperfect character and grade others' character. It is probably the single most common reason people have an aversion to talking about and critiquing others' character. People may view recommendations for character improvement as a personal assault. Instead, deliver feedback on the person's character with the right intent, tone, and timing. Remember, everyone is sensitive, and we are all far from perfect.

We fail at demonstrating character just like we fail at everything else. Character is a working continuum, and it takes a long time to build and maintain character standing. Likewise, it takes only one digression to experience a setback. Even perceptions about our character cause us harm. So keep working on your character, protect it by living your values, and watch out for blind spots. Understanding character context and definitions is a must for the individual. Without an understanding, the individual develops blind spots and cannot cultivate character.

CHAPTER SUMMARY

1. Through the adoption and cultivation of basic leadership fundamentals, the individual forms individual leadership characteristics.
2. Living your values and using an adopted set of traits unique to you builds your character.
3. Character is critical, and there is no denying that leadership character is a performance differentiator.

CALL TO ACTION

1. How do you define your individual character? How does that compare with your leadership character?
2. As a leader, what character traits do you hope to embody? How can you further cultivate those traits in yourself?
3. Journal your answers to questions 1 and 2 today and then again at regular intervals in the future. Take note of how your answers evolve over time.
4. Identify leaders you admire. What character traits do they successfully demonstrate through their leadership? Which of those traits would you like to adopt for yourself?

CHAPTER 5

THE IMPORTANCE OF CHOOSING AND CULTIVATING VALUES

Values are the seeds of individual leadership character and require constant cultivation, care, and feeding. In this chapter, we explain the difference between traits and values. Also, we expand on the importance of values and how they apply to self-leadership.

Like the growth of an oak tree, values may change their form, but they strengthen with time. Let's start by defining values and differentiate between values and traits. Is there a difference? Yes. Values are people's fundamental beliefs. Values are our most important principles, and they guide our decisions and actions. Sound familiar? It should—decisions and actions are directly linked to personal accountability. So, in this sense, our values are associated with our accountability and vice versa.

Traits are more descriptive, distinguishing characteristics—a distinctive quality specific to a person. So, values are belief and principle-based, and traits are individual characteristics. Now that we know the difference between traits and values, let's go deeper into values.

"A highly developed values system is like a compass. It serves as a guide to point you in the right direction when you are lost."

—Idowu Koyenikan

What Are Your Values?

It is a bit of cold water in the face but write down your core values now. Keep the list to five core values or less. It should take less than one minute. If it takes you longer than a minute, you may not know your core values. That is OK; we will discuss values in detail, and you will have an opportunity to perform a small exercise at the end of this chapter to define your core values. This task is a forcing function to encourage thinking. There is a reason to focus on a short list; we cannot simultaneously live all values with excellence because there are hundreds to choose from.

a guiding beacon to your leadership journey, mean we do not have or honor other values; it is a way to stay focused on the things that are important to us. At this stage in my life, my core values are respect, self-belief, hard work, simplicity, and family. I will explain my core values, which I trust will provide ideas to choose yours.

Hard Work Pays the Best Dividends

There are different values, such as physical, personal, and psychological. We will begin the discussion with the most critical physical value: hard work. Few people can achieve true success without hard work. Sure, some people achieve success without working hard—it is possible, but not likely.

Hard work allows a person to duplicate success time after time. There are many reasons to embrace it as a core value. Working hard builds character, competence, and resilience. It is proven that hard work outdistances talent. Learn to work hard, and success is only a matter of time.

Hard work reveals what we do well and what we need to improve. When working hard, the frustration you might feel is merely feedback that you need to improve on a specific area. Most folks get frustrated at the sign of hard work; this is a sure sign of someone who does not grasp delayed gratification. Hard work does not guarantee an outcome; it assures the opportunity for your desired outcome. You will have long days, late nights, and long weekends in the quest for any endeavor worth pursuing. Enjoy the ride, as hard work will get you to the destination. Work hard and love the journey.

Values go deeper than the surface. Values are more about inner meaning than superficial perspective. One example is the regard for a person's positioning versus all the hard work and struggles it took to get there. We must look deeper than the surface to learn the values that supported their accomplishment.

As a sophomore, Michael Jordan, arguably the greatest basketball player ever, did not make the high school team as he was a raw and undersized athlete. Yet, Jordan practiced tirelessly and made the team the following year. Over his junior and senior years, Jordan averaged twenty-five points per game and received a scholarship to North Carolina University.

Jordan developed determination at the University of North Carolina, and he was the number three overall pick by the Chicago Bulls. One year, the media criticized Jordan for not being a "defensive" player. So, what did Jordan do? He worked on his defensive game the entire off-season. The following year, Jordan won the NBA's most valuable defensive player award. Jordan refused to allow others to define his success. He overcame through the core value of hard work. People want to believe that Jordan succeeded off talent alone. Not at all—Jordan's hard work core value made the difference.

Kurt Warner, the former quarterback for the St. Louis Rams and Arizona Cardinals, is a second example. He started his journey to the Pro Football Hall of Fame as a third-string quarterback at the University of Northern Iowa. Warner's path was fraught with setbacks between Northern Iowa and the NFL Pro Football Hall of Fame. The Green Bay Packers cut Warner; he was relegated to the Arena Football League, cut from the St Louis Rams, relegated to NFL Europe, cut from the New York Giants, and cut from the St. Louis Rams again, where he had won a Super Bowl.

Finally, Warner completed his career with the Arizona Cardinals, where he led them to a Super Bowl and lost. Despite all the setbacks he experienced, Kurt Warner credits persistence and hard work as the values of his success. He never quit because he believed in the value of hard work. His success proved the value of hard work—an essential value to winning despite setbacks.

One need not always look to pro sports for examples of hard work. How about the soccer mom, single mom, or homemaker who never misses shuttling kids to practice while keeping up with all the household chores? Likewise, some single moms are also career professionals. Yet, they do not miss a beat. They know their hard work will pay off by creating opportunities for their children. Why do they do the seemingly impossible? They believe in the value of hard work. Moreover, they set an example.

My mom was a homemaker, and not just inside the home. My dad worked overseas a lot when I was young; it was me, my sister, and later my brother. For six to nine months, my mom took care of us, a house, and two acres of yard. We did not have a riding lawn mower either, so it was all push mower. I swear, I rarely saw her sit, and we did not sit much either, especially when we were old enough to help.

My mom signified strength to me, and she is the hardest worker I have ever known, hands down. We never missed a practice, always had the basics, and she put us before herself. In our house, if you joined sports, martial arts, or any team, you would show up for practice and games, no questions asked. And you did not come home complaining about practice or that you did not get this or that opportunity. The recurring refrain was "work harder."

How often have you traveled somewhere and got lost or stopped just one turn short of your destination? Then you realized if you had gone just a little further, you would have arrived at your intended objective. Hard work is the same; keep going a little longer and work just a little harder. You will arrive, and you will make your opportunity happen. WORK HARD.

Family Means More than the People You Are Related To

Family is a personal core value. I grew up in a small family around a larger extended family in southern Louisiana. We had cousins, in-laws, and the like in a five-mile stretch of road, and there were always large gatherings. My blood relatives were many in my neighborhood, as my family stemmed from seven brothers and six sisters on my father's side of the family. Yes, my grandmother had five sisters and seven brothers. In the Parish we lived in, large families were commonplace.

Across the Parish, there were large families and even larger extended families. Everyone had lots of cousins. Throughout my life and leadership journey, I have noticed that I seek these types of environments—a family atmosphere. It is as if I have always been searching for a tribal belonging. The Marine Corps fit my family core value perfectly.

Along my thirty-four-year leadership journey, I have seen folks who came from broken homes, no homes, and the like. But just as we can build a leader, we can build a family and accept people into our blood families. A good leader in an organization can create a family atmosphere. I have experienced this a few times in my thirty-four-year work career. Furthermore, I have tried to make the same family culture in the organizations and teams I was privileged to lead.

I have experienced adopting others as family in the Marine Corps and in private business. Marines are a close-knit group by necessity. One of the endearing qualities of the Marine Corps fire team, squad, platoon, and company is the tendency to close ranks when attacked by outsiders. The family value is the same. People come together during times of crisis and when family members are in need. Families, blood or not blood, put differences aside and take on the need to protect the family.

Think of the family as a tribe. People lived in close-knit bands and tribes for thousands of years, but blood relations did not define tribe membership or inclusion. That is the essence of the value of family.

Family, as a core value, builds self-leadership with respect to compassion and loyalty. When we interact with relatives or folks who we adopt into our family, we gain experience and perspective on the power of compassion and loyalty. We share in the struggle and distress of others; therefore, we learn how to lead with compassion. In turn, we reinforce those traits in our self-leadership journey. We are more likely to convey compassion and loyalty outside the family.

Believing in Yourself Takes Work

Believing in yourself is a psychological value. It has many benefits and is essential to your success. The more competent you are and the more character you build, the more likely you will believe in yourself. Competence takes practice at a task, job, or quality. Character takes an extreme level of effort to build each day. Therefore, it is essential to build competence and character ahead of self-belief. You may ask, *Why?* Character and competence make up trust, and you cannot believe in yourself if you do not trust yourself. Likewise, it takes hard work to master anything, and self-belief is no different.

Let's reach back to our leadership traits and discuss decisiveness. Do we believe we are decisive about everything when we are eighteen years old and on our own? Not close. Life gives us many decision-making dilemmas when we go out into the world with no measurable experience. There may be people who have a sixth sense about making decisive decisions at a young age; however, I would argue that it takes meaningful repetition of decision-making for most of us to become decisive.

Once we learn to be decisive, we have more confidence, and when we have more confidence, we will believe in ourselves. Building competence and confidence across tasks, job duties, and leadership enable us to believe in ourselves genuinely. Meaningful repetitions are essential to meet or exceed a standard of competence. Believing in yourself lays the groundwork for discipline in your life. If you believe you can do something, you will be more likely to have the will and commit to the desire or goal. Believing in yourself is a critical component of self-leadership. Without self-belief, we will not realize our full self-leadership potential because it takes belief to support and cultivate our traits and values.

Keep It Simple

Let's discuss the core value of simplicity. Simplicity is something we naturally seek as we mature. Believe it or not, life does not get more straightforward as we grow old. On the contrary, life gets complicated. So, naturally, we seek simplification, which takes time and effort.

We create a psychological picture of how things should be without all the complexity. Even if it is worked this long, just the way I am doing it, can I strip down the task, process, or job? When simplifying, it can feel uneasy to communicate straightforwardly, either verbally or in writing. It works, however. Once we put it into practice, the apprehension slowly subsides, and we realize that people are more responsive to simple communications.

There is power in simplification. When we can execute a task simply, it frees up time for work and allows us to focus on other higher priority items. Likewise, simplicity promotes speed and ease of work. Think about the things you do the most each day. I am willing to bet that most, if not all, of the tasks are simple in nature—people like simple, and it works. The main contribution of simple to the self-leadership journey is it frees time to focus on other tasks that require a higher level of concentration. In essence, by embracing simplicity you can give yourself time back.

Respect Is the Root of All Values

Let's bookend this chapter with the most important value of all: Respect. Respecting yourself and others is essential to all other values. Without respect, it is not easy to build and maintain rapport. Also, respect is the foundation of each kind of relationship.

Respect, like unselfishness, is easily recognizable and speaks volumes about an individual's character. So, what exactly is respect? Respect is showing regard or consideration. We respect our parents because they raise us into adults and look out for our best interests. Likewise, we respect our elders as they have more experience than we do.

We might show respect for someone highly accomplished in their field or career. That is how we show regard. The other component of respect, consideration, is the area I believe is the absolute most important, yet people wrestle with it more than displaying regard. Showing concern for things we do not have in-depth knowledge about is challenging yet important—for instance, another person's culture or beliefs. Too often, we allow bias to ruin our consideration of other societies and viewpoints.

Showing consideration does not mean you believe the same things or embrace other cultures; it means you show respect for things that are different. Respecting different things is the first step to looking deeper and learning about other people and their backgrounds. After some study and understanding, you might realize most people are more alike than different. Showing consideration allows people to coexist with minimal conflict over sensitive issues. Respect reinforces your credibility and improves your social bank account. People are more likely to come to you if they know you are a person who extends respect impartially with genuine consideration.

Values Change with Time and Circumstance

Core values can and will change over time. It does not mean we no longer honor the value; we adapt to our experiences and the things that are important to us. As we make our way in the world and establish different relationships, such as work, extracurricular, spousal, and community, we expose ourselves to more of life's lessons. Similarly, when folks retire, values can change. Society lays down expectations that might influence values as well.

CHAPTER SUMMARY

1. Values guide your compass to self-leadership.
2. Values can and will change over time.
3. Hard work always trumps talent.
4. All relationships start with respect, and self-respect is first.
5. Values drive our actions and decisions.

CALL TO ACTION

1. With an open mind and heart, reflect on your life experiences to date. List the values you have lived thus far.
2. Analyze your life environment (home life, school, work, extracurricular, etc.). What values are common to those environments?
3. Based on what you have experienced, what is important/ significant to you?
4. Based on your environment, what values allow you to succeed?
5. Of the values you have generated through the questions above, select the five values that are most important to you.
6. Perform a life inventory in which you reflect on how you have lived your top five core values at different stages of your life. Be as brutally honest with yourself as possible. How have you reflected or failed to reflect your values in each major period of your life? Were you able to maintain your values under criticism or in the face of temptation?

7. Considering your life inventory, think of ways you can better embody your core values going forward. Make a plan to become more mindful of those values and how you incorporate them into your daily life. Remember, your values should drive and influence actions and decisions in your life.

CHAPTER 6

SELF-TRUST AND SELF-BELIEF

The Prerequisites to Commitment and Discipline

What does trust mean? Trust, as it relates to personal and interpersonal relationships, is defined as a belief in the reliability or truth in someone. Author Steven Covey goes deeper to describe trust: "Trust is equal parts of character and competence." A simple way to think about trust in context is that trust is behaviors and results. We must spend a lifetime earning trust from others. Likewise, we must continually develop our character and competence to grow and reach higher stages of trust.

Equally, we must achieve self-trust. Self-trust is the very root of discipline. Without discipline, we cannot genuinely cultivate traits and values that are the backbone of self-leadership.

Self-trust is the hardest to earn. Self-belief, or the belief in your abilities and judgments, is underpinned by trusting yourself. With strong self-belief, we can aggressively pursue our interests and recover quickly from setbacks. However, without solid self-belief, we avoid challenges and lose confidence when we fail.

"Trust opens up new and unimagined possibilities."

—Robert Solomon

We have coupled self-trust and self-belief as we cannot have belief without trust. This chapter will cover perspectives on self-trust, trust-building, and how to combat the thoughts and actions that present barriers to and erode self-trust. We will also cover self-belief and its relationship to trust, as well as concepts, such as who you are versus what you are and building competency in your field.

Trust Yourself First

As odd as it may seem to some of you, we have a relationship with ourselves. It is no different from external relationships; the main difference is that we cannot successfully lie to or fool ourselves, which is a reality we must confront. Lying to ourselves is the absolute worst lie—attempting to do so erodes self-trust and self-belief and shatters confidence. So how can we maintain the conviction, coolness, and specific attributes of confidence with overwhelming self-doubt? Like they say, "that dog does not hunt."

People generally trust us because we are highly qualified in a specific area, have high character, or both. Businesses love true, subject-matter experts; they are the "go-to" people who can weigh in on particular problems. Subject-matter experts shape processes and procedures with vast knowledge.

We have all heard the term *trusted resource*. We naturally gravitate to people who keep their word and are reliable when we need them. We earn trust by keeping our word and executing tasks, projects, or jobs well. Therefore, we build trust through transactions—by making agreements and making good on them time after time. Trust building is a repetition of character and competence, but we must also transact genuinely because the more genuinely we interact with people, the deeper the trust we build.

Aside from interpersonal trust in business, the same holds true for keeping promises to ourselves. When we keep agreements with ourselves, we earn self-trust. Likewise, we erode self-trust when we do not follow through with our actions. Eroding self-trust is debilitating to the individual. Like it or not, self-trust is related to integrity. We are doing the right thing when no one is looking. No one knows most of our personal goals and promises to ourselves. However, we do, and that is something we cannot outrun. Learning to trust oneself comes from repetitively following through on a task, keeping promises to ourselves, and making good decisions when we know what is right.

We build self-trust by knowing our job. A good template for building competence in your job is learning it, performing it, teaching it, and writing about it. Each takes different experiences and skills. Learning and performing come first, followed by teaching and writing. The proper training for any job is critical. It might be on-the-job training or a mix of theoretical and on-the-job training. Each has its merit. Even when we teach, we learn. I have found that teaching provides a richer insight into any job. It reveals just what we know and what we do not know.

Earning Trust is Difficult

Do we consistently earn trust when we are competent and display good character? Unfortunately, we do not. Things happen: a bad performance, misunderstood intent, and dealing with people who do not trust themselves. We all have bad performances despite our best efforts. Take a pro sports team. One week they look like all-stars, and the next, they cannot get out of their own way. We can break this down into schemes, technical failings, effort, and sometimes the wild card of self-doubt. No matter what level we are at, we can experience self-doubt. Bright lights bring it out. The key is to move on from a bad performance and keep a short memory.

Again, if we try enough and dare enough, poor performance and failure are almost unavoidable. Move on; there is no utility in carrying around an awful performance. Sometimes we may struggle with communicating our intent. We make decisions and take action without speaking to the right people ahead of time. Instead, share the intent clearly and early.

Trust is the currency of leadership and self-leadership. My experience in sports, martial arts, the US Marine Corps, private business, contract services, and a Fortune 100 company provided a broad view of many trust environments. The people, teams, and organizations with the highest level of trust moved more swiftly and achieved more, hands down. The trust in a team or organization is the aggregate of people in the company and functions as a chain.

Like some links in a chain, there are strong and weak links. I have been in an organization where five teams depended on one another. Because of two people, the trust among the teams eroded to the point where we could not effectively deliver to our customers. Trust is aggregate, yet a few bad actors can ruin trust because of their character and competence issues.

Trust can be misunderstood, not easy to acquire, and we must maneuver rough ground to get it. By and large, people demand constant trustworthiness, yet they fail to trust themselves. So, what are they asking for, exactly? More often, people try to look at the right and wrong ways to trust rather than considering what framework they are extending trust. That brings us to the focus of this discussion—self-trust.

So how can we build and nurture self-trust? Self-trust at its crux is keeping promises to yourself. However, there are many effective ways to build self-trust. Enforce your personal boundaries, such as your values. Living up to a value means you value what is important to you enough to stand on it and act or not act.

For example, say one of your core values is courage. When presented with a risky situation, you will exhibit courage because you are committed to it. Your commitment to the value reinforces your self-trust. Building competence in your field or completing specific tasks reinforces self-trust. The better you get at doing something, the more you trust you can do it. Ask an expert; they trust themselves. Getting to know and trust and practicing the activities that bolster trust carry over to trust in your external relationships. How? You learn to recognize traits of trust in others: competence, living values, and strong character.

Trust Is Tricky

There are plenty of trust pitfalls. How often are we asked to trust others and ourselves when we do not have all the evidence or information about the situation? Extending trust with incomplete information introduces risk to trust. In relationships, disappointment and betrayal are part and parcel of the trust game.

How often have we had all the information but were too lazy to think and drive out inaccuracies that could have prevented misplaced trust? We are human, and it happens. We need to be judicious with our trust and use trust wisely.

Moreover, we need to recognize trusts, such as trust, distrust, and trustworthiness. Sometimes we trust people in promises that they make good on the trust. We want to believe they are trustworthy based on their track record or competence.

One example is a mental health advisor or doctor. We may not know their complete background, but we consider them trustworthy. We believe these professionals are trustworthy because their cause is noble, and they must demonstrate some level of competency to hold a license to practice their profession.

Still, some folks are untrustworthy. Be smart with your trust. Untrustworthy people constantly blame others, know too much, share too little, and have a track record of being unreliable. I cannot pretend that this is an exhaustive list; however, that is not the point. The point is that untrustworthy people behave in patterns. Patterns of behavior are always the differentiator between trustworthy and untrustworthy people. Be smart, objective, and look for behavior patterns.

Trust, like other values, can be hard to define, but you know it when you have it. Likewise, when we breach trust, it does not feel right. People see trust through different lenses. Some gravitate toward reliability and assurance of people. Others see it as character and competence. Some even say trust is following through with what you say you will do.

Solid character will always trump competence. Indeed, it is essential to maintain a high level of competency. Yet, your character is usually the differentiator in individual performance. People are more forgiving if we fall short in the competence component of trust, as we can continually improve skills with more time and training. Skills come and go, but our character remains and follows us throughout life.

We can improve on character; we all do as we mature and learn. However, it takes longer to rebuild character than competence. Display questionable character and folks keep it in memory for a long time. Constantly attacking others, being unreliable, and sharing confidential information about others are all examples of questionable character. These behaviors cause others to mistrust. Conversely, coming through in the crunch, time after time and maintaining confidentiality engenders trust. Dealing with others in the right way reinforces strength of character and therefore self-trust.

Self-Belief Follows Self-Trust

Self-doubt is the self-belief killer. Again, we are all human and experience some element of self-doubt. The level at which we allow self-doubt is wholly up to the individual. The key is to drive out self-doubt and resist the temptation to let it creep in. The best way to eliminate self-doubt is to remember your past accomplishments, do not compare yourself to others, and seek your validation instead of others'. Think of the times you succeeded in the face of doubt. Everyone achieves something in the face of challenges. No matter how small, overcoming any challenge is something to stand on. It builds confidence.

Likewise, comparing ourselves to others is a losing proposition. The yardstick is long in both directions; we are always better than some and not as good as others in any one endeavor. Measure yourself against the goals you set for yourself. Validation from others is not necessary; your accomplishments are different and are unique to you. Focus on your pathway to your end goal. This removes the thought of how others have achieved and prevents assessing your achievements against others. When presented with bad odds, it is time to purge self-doubt. When faced with bad odds, we must carry the winning mindset; we must believe we can overcome and win.

Self-belief is a person's faith in their capability to accomplish tasks or get things done. The more we decide and commit to performing a specific task or interface personally, the more self-belief we accumulate.

I have almost always believed in myself, but I have had times when my self-belief waivered. Over time, I have learned that specific things hold us back from self-belief. I looked at everyday things that held me back from solid self-belief. I had to release control of certain things, learn to be vulnerable, leave bad relationships, and accept responsibility for all my emotions and actions. It is all about control; we either have it, or we do not. Sometimes not having control is disconcerting.

Alternatively, when we are in control, we feel safer. That is a fact. Yet, what are we really in control of? Personal behavior is about the long and short of the matter. As for the balance of our lives, we are sharing control, or we have no control. As a man, sometimes it is difficult to show vulnerability. It is not about being macho, but rather, for some, it is what we were taught or exposed to in our formative years. We must be okay with sharing control and maintaining control of our emotions. We believe in ourselves if we understand and maintain control. Constantly giving in to emotions—an impulse—causes limited self-belief.

Distrust and previous encounters can cause us to lose the ability to trust. No trust, no vulnerability. However, we grow when we learn to trust and allow ourselves to be vulnerable. Easier said than done. Show me your circle, and I will show you your future—so true. As harsh as it may sound, if our closest friends, colleagues, and family do not improve, we must distance ourselves from them. We benefit from people who genuinely want to see us succeed in our endeavors.

Above all, I believe that the ability to take ownership of our emotions and actions leads to the strongest self-belief. Owning your actions and feelings lead to the ability to cope with and succeed under stress. We know that stress is part of life. The more we dare greatly, the more vast the stress.

Setbacks take time to recover; your self-belief will return with enough hard work and commitment. Rebuilding self-belief is like repairing a broken object. You need to assess the damage, fix it accordingly, and return the thing to some serviceable condition. Repairing self-belief is no different. The key is to honestly assess why your self-belief suffered a setback in the first place.

Most notably, self-belief leads to confidence. Once I learned to trust and believe in myself, I learned how to truly commit to essential things; in turn, my ability to maintain confidence and discipline increased. My performance at work improved, and so did my relationships. Constant evaluation/improvement of character and competence are required to sustain self-trust and self-belief, which are powerful enablers and lay the groundwork for commitment and discipline.

CHAPTER SUMMARY

1. Trust in self is first—We cannot trust others if we do not trust ourselves first.
2. Earning trust is difficult—We must continually work on our competence and character to earn higher levels of trust.
3. Self-belief follows self-trust—The more faith we put in our abilities, the more we build self-trust.

CALL TO ACTION

1. Create a daily or weekly list of tasks you hope to accomplish. Then do them! Setting and accomplishing goals is the first step to cultivating trust in yourself.

2. If you have made promises to yourself—even small ones—share them with someone close to you. Ask that person to help hold you accountable.

3. Guard against self-doubt by remembering your past accomplishments. Make a list of times you have been proud of yourself and return to that list anytime you experience a setback.

4. Practice self-belief by taking responsibility for your actions. Do not make excuses!

CHAPTER 7

COMMITMENT AND DISCIPLINE DRIVE PERSONAL RESPONSIBILITY

I have always gravitated to structure. I believe my first exposure to structure outside of the house was American football. Practice every day, learn plays, learn commitment and discipline, and learn to show up. American football is a simple game of schemes. It is highly structured. I learned structure at home by doing schoolwork, chores, and the like. I always showed up for sports, military, and martial arts and had the discipline to do the small things without fail.

I enjoyed football and martial arts practice just as much as the Friday night lights or the big Tae Kwon Do tournament. However, there is nothing like scoring a touchdown or placing first in a contest. Scoring a touchdown is a team effort; however, the individual must do their part. Scoring points and ranking high are validation of hard work and effort. Most importantly, it represents commitment and discipline.

Commitment and discipline mean different things to different people. In the context of this book, we define the terms as follows: commitment is a guarantee or a promise that we will do something.

Some folks may describe commitment as a covenant common to marriage and business. In this light, commitment has a heavy meaning. Indeed, commitment requires a decision. We must decide before committing to an action, task, or endeavor. During that decision is when we should recognize the weight of the decision and the level of commitment required to hold up the promise and guarantee. We guarantee our effort, as we do not have crystal balls, and we cannot guarantee outcomes.

Commitment is not compliance. Compliance is *I must do it*, whereas commitment is *I want to do it.* Think of taxes, for example. Although the taxes contribute to the greater good of everyone, most people wait until the filing deadline. That is compliant behavior. On the other hand, commitment is different. A committed person will do whatever it takes—and as soon as practical—to achieve a goal or make good on a promise. When people want to do something, there are very few boundaries they cannot overcome. I have seen it many times.

My sister is an example. She started college when she was in the tenth grade. She went on to earn a Rotarian scholarship to study abroad, and when she returned, she had a scholarship to a university. My parents could not afford college, nor would they have paid for it if they had had the money. You had to earn everything at our house.

My sister chose to pursue medicine and become a physician, but she had to make enough money to start medical school. She began in environmental sales with zero experience but quickly became a top seller. She wanted it—she stayed committed. After applying to medical school, she was not accepted at any domestic universities, so she went to a medical school in the Caribbean. There was no air conditioner for most of her school, and she was alone with no friends or family. She did not complain. She wanted to do it, and she graduated with honors. She is the epitome of commitment.

She liked the medical field, decided to pursue it, and stayed committed and disciplined. As a result, she has a private medical practice, teaches medical classes at the university, and is vice president of her hospital. She dominates in a male-dominated field. Throughout my sister's life, she has been the epitome of commitment to her practice. Without a steel commitment, great goals and desires cannot be achieved or outcomes realized. With consistent commitment, we assure self-leadership improvement because we have pledged to improve.

Discipline Is the Gateway to Success

"Discipline equals freedom."

—Jocko Willink

Discipline, like commitment, takes on many definitions and is most mistaken for the regimen. The two are markedly different. Discipline is to obey with consistency—to decide, commit, and obey each time. We follow laws, rules, personal boundaries, and good habits. We must abide by our own rules if we consider ourselves disciplined. If I set a goal of working out each day, I must obey that self-imposed rule each time without fail, or I fall short of discipline.

Discipline does not mean perfect. As stated, life happens, and external factors/emergencies can influence our daily grind. If I miss a workout because I had to go to the emergency room, that does not mean I fell short of discipline. If I miss a workout because I had a late day at work and did not get my training in, then I am not disciplined, even if it is late. I had a chance to get it in, but I did not make the time. Know the difference and do not split hairs between *I do not have time* and *I do not make time.*

The best workouts I have had are when I am dog-tired. Get your workout in. Discipline is the root of self-leadership. Think of discipline as a foundation. All other pillars of self-leadership stand on discipline. Discipline assures that we commit to the things that are important to us time after time.

I have always committed to showing up for football and martial arts. I played football for twelve years and never missed a practice—fifteen years of martial arts without missing a practice on purpose. I loved football practice, and I never minded the constant feedback loop. I wanted to do better. Although I must admit I never had a coach holler at me. I tried my hardest every practice. I cannot even say wind sprints sucked. Although, yes, my lungs burned, and my ass cheeks and thighs felt like rubber; somehow it never broke my spirit. To me, it was competition and an opportunity to get better.

My mom would always say do not let anyone outwork you or outrun you. She was a master at psychology and knew what made me tick. She knew I was not the fastest, and I soon learned that I was not slow by any means. Her point was to instill the value of discipline and hard work. Few would outwork me because I loved football, and I was 100 percent committed.

Football is where I learned many types of discipline. I jumped offsides twice in my twelve-year football career. I was embarrassed, and it never happened again. I always watched the ball—except for those two times. I played running back briefly and learned that I needed eye discipline not to give away the hole I would run through. As a tight end, if my split was too close to the tackle, the defense might know it was a run. All these little things take discipline.

Consistency Makes the Difference

I must reiterate the word *consistency*. Consistency is not sexy and sometimes may feel mundane. However, the payout comes from the everyday consistency required to maintain discipline. The boring feeling you might get during mundane tasks is building habits; it is incremental. It is like working out; we do not get the gains immediately; it takes time.

Working out is laborious and mundane. We pick the weights up and set them down. Not exactly a party, but if you like it, it is just ordinary and not a drag. How about learning kicks in any martial arts? It takes thousands and thousands of kicks to do it without hesitation and execute the kick well. The spinning heel kick must be the one people need the most repetitions to master. The individual must pivot, take their eyes off the target, spin, find the target again, and hit the mark with the small part of their heel. Never mind, keep your balance too. Practice this kick wrong, and you will do it exactly how you practiced it. The spinning heel kick takes inordinate commitment and discipline to master.

Consistency and discipline are the same.

Trust, Self-Belief, and Commitment Underpin Discipline

Like a house, discipline requires a solid foundation to stand firmly—trust, self-belief, and commitment. Lose any of these, and you will not sustain discipline. It is the key to maintaining discipline, which many people misunderstand. Two big examples are failing at fad diets and habit breaking, which always result from a combination of losing trust, self-belief, or commitment.

Moreover, half-hearted decisions play a leading role too. For example, the infamous new year's resolution or quitting the gym. How many times have you seen people carry out new year's resolutions? I do not believe many people ever carry out their New Year's resolutions to the letter, and I have personally seen people quit gyms in less than two weeks. Why does this happen? Misinformed, shaky decisions and the absence of the disciplined building-block concept are the roots of the failures. Folks try to short-circuit the path to discipline without belief and commitment.

I have simplified the reasons people cannot sustain discipline. There are other factors. Folks are usually committed and disciplined to things that interest them. But isn't the goal to maintain discipline in those things that do not interest us if it plays a role in self-fulfillment or enrichment? Yeah, it might suck but so what? Daring greatly requires some risk and a whole lot of discipline.

To acquire anything of value or meaningful enrichment takes hard work, commitment, and discipline. If you really want something, you must work hard and maintain discipline all the time—not some of the time. You have not dared enough if you achieve the goal without hard work, commitment, and discipline. Pursue something more significant and scarier. I promise you will be pleasantly surprised that you can rise to new levels by genuinely committing to a meaningful endeavor.

If you struggle with consistency in difficult tasks, think back to what desire or goal you have set for yourself. If you struggle with consistency, the desire or goal may not be strong enough for you. Likely, you have prioritized the goal or desire beneath others you are currently pursuing.

Likewise, why give difficult a vote? Break down difficult tasks into smaller, achievable ones and count the small wins. Look at how you attack difficult tasks. What course of action are you taking? Is there room to simplify? Alternatively, if you are struggling with consistency in the mundane tasks of life, then it is a matter of perspective. Stop seeing the tasks as mundane and, rather, as smaller pieces of the overall mission that are, in fact, important. When you can establish consistency in what you thought was mundane, you win.

Personal Accountability

It all boils down to personal accountability. The root of personal responsibility starts with being honest with yourself. Take ownership of your decisions, actions, and situation. Do not blame others for your shortfalls. However, external factors are real; focus on what you can control and influence. Be honest with what you can manage and accept that you may influence very little, if anything, in most situations.

Drive out the wishful thinking. Focus on what you actually can control and influence, which will eliminate assigning responsibility to others if a failure occurs. Failure is almost inevitable. If you are not failing, you are not trying enough. Likely you are overperforming and underachieving.

Commitment takes us to the decision to act. Leadership is about action, but we must get ourselves to a place where we are ready to act. We cannot act decisively if we are half-hearted about something meaningful. A strong commitment means we are making space for something meaningful. In the self-leadership framework, commitment is a pillar of discipline. With strong-rooted commitment that underpins discipline, we will maintain personal accountability.

CHAPTER SUMMARY

1. Discipline requires the prerequisites of self-belief, trust, and commitment.
2. We truly commit to the things we love.
3. Personal accountability is a by-product of owning your decisions and actions.

CALL TO ACTION

1. Evaluate commitments you have made in the past. How often did you remain successfully committed? When did you fail? Try to identify factors that contributed to that success or failure.

2. To what in your life do you *commit*? To what in your life do you simply *comply*? Are there any noticeable differences between the two groups? How do you reconcile this?

3. Think of a time in your life when you showed great discipline. What drove you?

4. If you are someone who struggles to maintain consistency in your actions, try charting your progress. Set a goal and document how well you adhere to it. If you start slipping, try to identify reasons for backsliding. Recognizing a pattern is the first step to overcoming it.

CHAPTER 8

STAYING SOVEREIGN

What are you willing to endure to be known as someone who lives their values? If our values are the most important things to us, are we not obligated to live them all the time? Living your values at any cost is not easy—it means you have the resolve to stand for something. After all, if we are not willing to live our values, what is the point? Do we wander through life going with the flow, selecting self-preservation at each turn, or do we choose to stay sovereign on our values and the things that matter most? Are you willing to step up and speak up? We must step up, speak up, and stay sovereign on what matters most to us. Staying sovereign builds leadership character, demonstrates strong commitment to values, and comes with a personal and social cost.

What Is Sovereignty?

What is the definition of sovereignty? Let's look at a few different meanings and examples of sovereignty to get perspective. Likely, most people think of state or national sovereignty, economic sovereignty, or someone who has ultimate decision rights for the whole of a state. For example, America is a sovereign nation financially and physically. In contrast, remember Greece a few years back, the country became insolvent and had to depend on a bailout from the EU. The bailout cost Greece its economic sovereignty. Bailouts and loans always come with control measures and strings attached. The leaders of Greece yielded sovereignty because they made terrible financial and economic decisions.

Freedom from external control is another viewpoint. The dictionary says sovereignty is a self-governing state. Financial sovereignty means that your debt, if any, is manageable, and you are not under the control of overextended credit. You have savings to fall back on in hard times. Physical sovereignty means you have the means to protect your property and person. For example, you may have fenced property to keep folks out, an alarm system to warn of threats, and you may have specialized training to defend yourself should the need arise. You get the point; sovereignty is the authority to maintain control of decisions and avoid undue influence from external forces. In short, you have a level of autonomy over your life.

"Eagles fly above the fray."

—Bobby Harrington

Stand Up for Your Beliefs

So how do we relate sovereignty to leading self? First, we can stand for the truth and live our values. We make our own decisions based on our value system. We keep our values and standards *sovereign* through our actions—by standing up for what we believe in. The key is that when you are sovereign, you stand for your values all the time and not some of the time.

Sovereignty is often misunderstood as stubbornness. For example, people who have convictions get labeled as stubborn rather than sovereign. They will not budge. Their convictions to live their values drive them to stand firm in what they believe in no matter what. People often think that someone is just being hardheaded; in truth, they are demonstrating the courage to resist undue external influence. Some people are willing to risk it all to stay sovereign.

We control how we live our values, and it is incumbent to speak up when our values do not match something people are trying to force on us—when our values are at risk. There are ways to convey that something does not match our values. Usually, you can share an impartial viewpoint based on what is right. You will be surprised at people's reactions when you stand up for your values and what you believe to be "the right thing." Most will respect you for it, especially if you logically deliver your dissent with some solid basis.

People will seek you when there is trouble and unfairness rears its ugly head. Become known for standing up for what you believe in, and in the long run, you will be glad you did. You will not have to look back and wonder what you stood for.

Sovereignty Builds Character

Leading self requires sovereignty on things that matter. Also, staying sovereign builds individual leadership character. As you exercise living values, it shapes how your leadership character develops. Remember that character is part of trust-building, so the more leadership character you build, the more you will trust yourself. The more you trust yourself, the more confident you will become.

For instance, staying sovereign on the value of respect for yourself and others instills something unique in your character. For one, you become comfortable exchanging and extending respect to all people. Secondly, you command respect; you do not demand it.

Commanding respect is a function of how you present yourself. When you command respect, you do not ask for it. When people *demand* respect, they must verbally ask for it, waiving their authority. Work at commanding respect by staying sovereign to your values.

What about staying sovereign to yourself? For some, this may be a foreign concept. If we can be outwardly sovereign to our values and the things that are important to us, we can look inward and do the same. Have you ever decided not to do a certain activity or make a particular choice because it does not align with your values? Then you find yourself in the middle of that exact activity or making that wrong choice? What pushed you to do it? Peer pressure, the path of least resistance, self-negotiation, temptation, all of the above? If so, you did not stay sovereign to yourself.

The next time this happens, make the right choice for you. Do not self-sabotage by caving into an impulse or short-term gratification. Caving in does not build sovereignty—it weakens your ability to stay true to yourself. Remember your values and attributes; cultivating those traits and values requires sovereignty.

Sovereignty Has a Cost

Sovereignty comes with a personal and social cost. The dichotomy of staying sovereign is the cost versus the gain. In most organizations, you will gain respect for speaking your truth and living your values. In some organizations, it can cost you promotions and result in marks on your performance reviews—sometimes, you might acquire the maverick label. So be it. I would rather be known for standing for something than falling or blindly following everything.

The status quo is the status quo; we do not move forward or backward. Dreadful. This circles back to leading self in a career and selecting self-preservation as a strategy. Choosing self-preservation as a strategy is the wrong career move. Yet we see it all the time.

There is a high cost to sovereignty—to yourself and others. Consider all these factors when choosing to remain sovereign. This book is about leading self, but we must mention that, as a leader, your sovereignty over values and decisions may affect anywhere from a few to millions of people.

It is okay to be the lone voice of dissent. Being the lone voice of dissent in discussions or meetings where groupthink has taken hold does not make you wrong. Just because everyone agrees on something does not make it right. On the contrary, if everyone agrees violently on critically important issues, something is likely wrong. Supporting the status quo gets the organization the status quo. A strong commitment to values marks highly effective people and organizations.

Most importantly, highly effective people and organizations do not settle for the status quo. In highly effective organizations, the revered people are the ones with solid values. People with solid values are the "balance" of an organization. People who are consistently sovereign make an organization stronger. People and organizations stay sovereign no matter the cost because it defines them. Moreover, they firmly believe staying sovereign benefits them and the organization. They know and believe that short-term cost is worth the long-term gain.

"It is dangerous to be right where established men are wrong."

—VOLTAIRE

In my last assignment with the integrated oil company I worked for, I had a high-level discussion with my new supervisor and his boss, an executive. It was my first week of a three-year assignment. My boss called me to the headquarter's building without advance notice of the subject matter. After sitting down in the executive's office, I discovered that the subject matter was the reliability and safety of process equipment. We had a high-pressure, gas-producing asset out of compliance, which was immediately dangerous to people, processes, and the environment. The discussion would center on the treatment of the out-of-compliance item.

There were two options; let the asset continue to operate unsafely or shut down the asset for remedial repairs. After twenty-eight years in the field, I knew that this would be the most important meeting of my assignment, as it would set the tone for my value boundaries. It would test my sovereignty.

The group indirectly asked me to look the other way and agree to allow the asset to maintain a dangerous operating condition. Shutting down the asset severely impacted oil production and therefore lost revenue. After explaining the value of safe operating equipment, I held to my values of safety over oil production. I stated that I could not support continued operation under unsafe conditions in a relaxed and calm manner. I could have agreed to allow the asset to run to failure per the executive's wishes; however, there was a greater need to stay sovereign. People, equipment, and the environment are more valuable than barrels of oil.

I did gain a label from that conversation and many more after it, yet it never bothered me because it was the right thing to do. Conversely, I gained the respect of the people I was leading at the time because I represented the values of the safety program. The remainder of that three-year assignment would be more of the same. In this example, my boss and executive made the right decision. Once again in my career, I earned the maverick title, and I would battle against that perception for the remainder of the assignment.

Staying sovereign on values when there is pressure to waiver is easy and difficult. The easy part is you know what to do—the hard part is how to deliver it in such a way as to preserve your relationships and credibility. Personally, I am direct about it because I am a believer in preserving life and assets. Staying sovereign when it mattered only strengthened my resolve and self-leadership capabilities.

Sovereignty Applies to Feelings and Emotions

Everyone has feelings and emotions, and we all manage them differently. In relationships, we keep firm on the emotions and feelings we are willing to reveal until we extend and earn trust. We do cede our feelings and emotions to those we trust and love. We are less sovereign with people we love, and sometimes that comes with a cost.

People take advantage when our guard is down, and we might be vulnerable. You know the sting if you have ever been screwed over or taken advantage of by a lover, friend, or colleague. After we are taken advantage of, we become sovereign again, and we are more judicious with feelings and emotions. We are also less likely to be vulnerable around those who hurt us. We become sovereign.

CHAPTER SUMMARY

1. Staying sovereign on things that matter comes with a personal and social cost.
2. Staying sovereign builds self-leadership character.
3. Do not allow peer pressure or your lack of discipline to drive you to sacrifice your beliefs for gain.
4. Protect your values and maintain autonomy over your decisions and actions. Do not let others make your decisions and force your actions.

CALL TO ACTION

1. Take a look back at the list of core values you identified in Chapter 4. When have you stood up for these values in your work or home life?
2. Were there times when you fell short in maintaining personal sovereignty, i.e., when you failed to defend your core values? How might you improve when similarly tested in the future?
3. After reading this chapter, write down one to three areas in your life where you should stay sovereign.

CHAPTER 9

THE THREE-PRONGED CAREER DILEMMA

Part of being a successful self-leader is recognizing when to focus on your job, when to seek balance in your job and career, and when to pursue career advancement. Do you focus on your job alone, your job and career, or only on advancing your career? The good news is that you can choose one path and have them all, but not all at once. Let me explain.

There are three modalities a person can pick during a career. First, you can choose to **do your job**; you can show up each day, make the most of training, know your job, build relationships, and get work done. Option two is you can choose to **do your job and focus on your career**. This option comes with trade-offs.

Even thinking about career advancement too much is destructive. You are renting mental space for your personal promotion and taking away focus from doing your job. The last option is to **focus solely on your career**. In this mode, it is all about you and your advancement and whatever it takes to find the next rung on the ladder. Do you think anyone reveres you for constantly trying to engineer your career? Note: projecting that you prioritize your career instead of doing your job is not a performance differentiator. Over the course of a career, we can do our job, do our job and advance our career, or try to advance our career exclusively; we cannot do all of them well.

If you grasped the point of the introduction, the best option is to focus on your job. This option provides a better possibility to achieve the career you desire. You might ask, "If I work hard, know my job, and get things done, will I advance?" You will. "If I do not focus solely on my career, won't my peers pass me?" They will not, and who cares? It would be best not to view your career as a race against others. Instead, measure your success against your expectations. Advancement is like understanding goal setting; it is incremental, and you must focus on the milestones ahead of you. The road is long.

What Is Promotion?

Is promotion purely the next position or pay grade? More money? It could be if that is indeed what you value. What about personal promotion? People who know their jobs and take care of other people promote themselves in the eyes of others, independent of the structural award that comes with the next position, pay grade, and money.

I have put a value on positioning, pay grades, and money, although I learned that personal promotion is worth more. I have more weight on personal promotion than money and positioning in an organization. Having the experience, behaviors, and skill to command respect means far more than any monetary salary or positioning in an organization. After all, we are but small pieces, forever moving in and out of the apparatus in most large organizations. Much like the military, we are a number in the system. With or without us, the machine continues to rattle and hum.

Placing more emphasis on relationships and commanding respect builds a more meaningful career and work experience. Reaching a point where you can command respect requires dedicated and disciplined self-leadership. Some people will not like you for doing your job, so please do not mistake their dislike for you for them not respecting you. Keep moving, and do not give them a second thought.

People always watch and emulate their leaders. People analyze how leaders lead themselves. In the same light, people observe you and your capacity to lead yourself. Here is where awareness and improvement will pay you dividends. Look at every interaction and every opportunity as a job interview. Each interaction is a chance to put on your best self-leadership performance. Be yourself and improve the rough spots. This does not mean people-pleasing and pandering to the status quo or someone else's agenda.

On the contrary, stay sovereign and push back where you believe it is in your best interest. People and leaders will try their best to manipulate others' thoughts and actions to suit their agenda. Let them know you are not okay with it. It is crucial to establish boundaries in your work environment. Most organizations encourage the go-along-to-get-along philosophy—conform to gain acceptance. Likewise, some people adopt this concept to avoid jeopardizing their sense of belonging. Few will challenge the status quo, which is no more than a correlation to groupthink. I encourage you to challenge where necessary and disrupt the status quo. You will be no worse for wear, and there are no changes to the status quo without individuals willing to challenge it.

Be Careful with Ambition, Competitiveness, and Ego

So, what drives us to try and manage to do our job the best we can and pursue a career simultaneously? And what causes us to focus solely on finding the next rung on the ladder? More often, I have found that it is ambition and competitiveness. Both, if allowed, will drive you to focus on your job/career and the myopic view of your career only. Unfortunately, I have not seen this work well many times. So, let's discuss ambition and competitiveness.

Ambition: the strong desire to achieve something. Likewise, hard work and determination follow ambition. Yet, we must not misplace ambition for laying waste to relationships, burning bridges, and personal destruction. I have seen many people allow ambition to get the best of them. It usually ends in burnout, depression, and loss of desire, which are often driven by the ego and validation.

According to the famous psychologist Freud, the human intellect has three dimensions. We have an Id ego, Ego, and a Super-Ego. In short, the Id is internal, formed at birth, and does not change throughout our lifetime. Whereas the Ego changes by effects of the outer world, and it is the decision-making part of the three ego dimensions. Ultimately, the Ego decides our behavior. The Super-Ego combines learned morals and values from home life. Likewise, it works in the conscious and preconscious and checks the Id's urges.

We operate in one or all the ego categories at any one time: conscious and unconscious. Usually, it is the Id that gets us in trouble. The Id is the rash part of the mind that reacts to urges. It causes urgent and direct responses to wants and wishes. Most importantly, the Id is where we find selfishness. If gone unchecked by the Super-Ego, the Id Ego gives way to impulse and aggression. If we are the sum of all our choices and actions, we must keep our egos in check. During a career, think of it as many micro choices that can guide us to the ego-ideal (the ideal balance between Id-Ego-Super-Ego).

People seek so much validation from outside of themselves in today's world. It is a constant self-measurement against external standards. I want to be like this; I want to have that; I wish I were like him/her. People give in to urges easily.

The quest for validation happens when people do not identify their values, live by them, and exercise self-control. They seek only external validation, which is dangerous because the standards on the outside are forever changing. Often folks who need all sorts of external validation have self-esteem problems. They fear rejection personally and in social settings. There is a way out of this rut. Treat rejection the same way as failure. Learn from it and move on. Often, the rejection is more about the other person or group rejecting you.

It does take some resilience to get past the fear of rejection. Ask yourself, *Why do I need to be accepted? Is acceptance something that makes me feel good temporarily?* More often than not, the answer is yes. As humans, we all want to be accepted; however, the reality is that not everyone or all social groups will accept us. Confront this reality and limit your expectations for external validation, and you are well on the way to more self-validation and a mentally stronger you.

Competitiveness can lead to negative relationships. Although well-intentioned, people view you as self-absorbed, picky, and passive-aggressive when you display harmful, competitive characteristics. Instead, compete within yourself. Set personal goals and use an internal measuring stick; this takes self-trust and commitment. Remember, trust and commitment are the pillars of discipline.

Always trying to keep up with others takes energy away from working on you. Remember that each thought and action compared to others is a tax on your personal development. Flip the script and make your thoughts and actions pay dividends in your development account.

If you struggle too much with failure, it signifies competitiveness. Do not get me wrong—it is okay to be a sore loser. No one likes the taste of losing. However, look at failure as a chance to rearm and do your best to get over it quickly. You can detect competitive people in conversations who always want to one-up another. One-upping is not constructive, although most do not realize they are doing it. It trivializes others' comments and lets the other party know you always need the last word. Save the one-upping for beer night or the fish story.

However, you can use ambition and competitiveness to achieve your career goals. Step back and think about how you apply ambition and competitiveness. Deploy your ambition with purpose and focus. Timing is everything. At the right time, ask for job opportunities with increasing responsibility. The right time is when you have mastered the role you are in, and you can confidently take on the challenges of the position you are seeking. Never ask for an opportunity out of your perceived entitlement because, quite frankly, you are not entitled to anything. Sorry.

There are times to focus on your career. Two to three discussions per year should suffice at most. There is no reason to run around each day trying to figure out your next assignment or the next promotion. Opportunities will come as a by-product of good work. Let the work you do speak for itself. Overachieve on tasks assigned to you that display your competency. If you work hard enough and long enough, someone will notice, and opportunities will present themselves. The opportunities driven by your hard work will satisfy your ambition.

It is okay to seek progression aggressively, yet let your performance be the mechanism. If you are doing your best to meet and exceed expectations, and you are not progressing, one or two things are happening: either you have a "bad boss," or you are in the wrong organization—possibly both. Make sure you are in the right organization where your talents are valued.

Celebrate and Cocreate

Be sure to celebrate other people's successes genuinely. At first, your competitiveness may not allow for it. However, over time, you will come to appreciate the achievements of others. You will appreciate their hard work and take away behaviors and approaches to aid in accomplishing your own success.

There have been times when I was too ambitious and competitive. I had to learn there is a time and place for everything. When I learned to deploy ambition and competitiveness in a way that served me best, my perception of success changed dramatically. Instead of being competitive, I worked to form collaborative relationships.

Strive to partner and cocreate. Co-creation provides a venue for the acceptance of different ideas and perspectives. Seek out opinions and allow ideas from peers, supervisors, and subject-matter experts. You will expand your sphere of influence and build your trust bank with these folks.

As leaders of others, we must lead ourselves first. People focused exclusively on careers make selfish and bad decisions. Take the politician leader who makes decisions based on serving his goals versus the organization's goals. How about the manager who thinks he is a leader and shits on everyone to advance his career? These people have the privilege to lead others, yet they cannot lead themselves effectively.

These people are in every business, sports franchise, military, and the like. They believe in the one-way feedback model. How can they grow as individuals without feedback? Two-way feedback is critical to building interpersonal relationships. Relationships without a two-way feedback loop will sour at some point. Eventually, criticism, contempt, stonewalling, and defensiveness creep into the relationship.

I reviewed an engineer's report one time ahead of a technical submission. When I delivered the feedback in writing and verbally, he got upset and turned red. I merely gave minor considerations for wording and a different perspective. He eventually stated that he disliked his work being criticized and hated the company. What? Yes, you will deal with highly sensitive people —even in the best of circumstances. My point is that feedback may be taken in many ways, no matter how it is delivered. And remember, treat all people as sensitive.

Do Your Job!

Focus on doing your job and performing it well. Lead yourself by building your competence through skill development. Skill development, like self-leadership, is a requirement at any career stage. Demonstrate soft-skill leadership traits. Communicate with intent and in a respectful delivery and tone. We must continually strive to get better.

With more experience, the skill-development gains are incremental. Every assignment takes a new you and some self-leadership focus. You will need to examine the leadership traits and decide which ones are critical to your success. For example, leading people in a high-risk environment requires unique self-leadership. Let's examine why leadership trait bearing is essential. Former coworkers would often say to me, "I cannot imagine you getting upset." Leading people in high-risk work requires people to demonstrate exceptional bearing. There may be micro and macro crises daily. Panic is the worst move a leader can make.

The team typically looks to one person in every high-pressure, high-risk situation. Sometimes it is the leader; other times, it may be an individual—it might be **you**. Risk desensitization occurs from operating in a high-risk environment for extended periods. People get used to the same conditions, and accidents become an acceptable part of the job. However, the accidents could have been prevented by recognizing and mitigating the likely part of the risk. Remember that risk is one part likelihood (probability) and one part consequence—an event or accident and a result. We usually control the likelihood part more than we control the consequence.

Leading yourself and doing your job is the best career strategy. It is all about where you spend your energy and focus. Embracing delayed gratification takes awareness and acceptance that anything worth attaining is complex and, most times, a rocky road. There are many dimensions and routes to navigate on the long road of a career. Indeed, the road is long, and we will contend with many challenges. Some are obstacles we must learn to negotiate, and some are self-made. We will do better to eliminate actual or imagined self-made barriers by checking our ego and resisting the impulse for short-term gain. Working hard at character and competence will yield more dividends than always seeking the next rung on the ladder.

CHAPTER SUMMARY

1. Promotion comes to us in many forms.
2. Constructively control your ambition and competitiveness.
3. Doing your job well is the best career path.

CALL TO ACTION

1. What are the benefits and drawbacks of focusing on excelling in your current job?
2. What are the benefits and drawbacks of devoting yourself to career advancement?
3. What are the potential benefits and drawbacks if you decide to do both simultaneously?
4. Record your responses to the questions above in your journal.
5. Additionally, consider how you are using ambition. Is it fueling you forward or simply feeding your ego?

CHAPTER 10

NOTHING IS PERFECT

I was an imperfect perfectionist for forty-five years, and once I accepted that people, life, and leadership were not perfect, it was a game changer. Have you ever known someone who overanalyzed things, even the simple things in life? Worse yet, someone who tried to act, do, and write perfectly? I was that person, and I never accomplished any of the three.

I started to examine how I perceived people, life, and leadership and how I approached matters mentally. I concluded that I had carried a trait passed down from my mother. She was a perfectionist in everything, and she was meticulous. You would never see dust on the furniture, an unvacuumed carpet, or anything out of place in the house. My mom expected maximum effort in all things all the time, perfect effort. In turn, I became indoctrinated to think the same way about most things. I did not make excellent grades, which was always a source of tension in our house. My older sister is a genius, so her performance measured me.

It was a strict upbringing with a parent who carried a perfectionist mindset. Little did I know that she intended to teach excellence and attention to detail, and she wanted better for us. I had the perfectionist mindset until I was forty-five years old; however, I was an imperfect perfectionist. People, life, and leadership are not perfect, so people should not get caught up in seeing leadership through a perfectionist's lens.

"Perfect is an illusion."

—Tucker Max

What Exactly Is Perfect?

Let's define and discuss a few different perspectives on *perfect*. Perfect most often means no flaws in an object or performance. Some may have an abstract view of perfect—the ideal person, gentleman, woman, or life. The dictionary provides similar definitions, such as meeting all requirements, situations, or states uninhibited from errors and blemishes. Having all qualities and characteristics as good as possible can describe perfect. Yet, the norms and definitions of perfect rarely occur. People often use the word *perfect* in response to something that meets their requirements or aspirations. We often hear people say, "perfect." Do they mean perfect? Probably not. I believe they mean "that satisfies my need."

Where do we see perfect show up in self-leadership and life? Perfect appears in personal habits, interpersonal behavior, self-leadership, planning, performance, image, and a host of other areas.

First, we must address why people seek out perfection. People want to believe things are perfect to reduce the chance of painful judgment and avoid shame. Likely, most people get inundated with many expectations that are not achievable. High expectations in all aspects of society cause people to ask themselves if they are enough. Soon after, they start the pursuit of perfection, and they find out perfect is an illusion and a shield.

There is no amount of mental or physical work that makes us perfect. We all have some minor physical and mental flaws. We are all flawed individuals, and our imperfections vary. Yet, people try to achieve perfection every day. It is hard to break the mental paradigm, primarily due to personal fear. People strive for perfection to mask personal flaws. They might think that if they try to look, act, and live ideally, somehow they might avoid judgment and feel more worthy.

You do not need to try to be perfect. You must stop and evaluate the energy you put into everything and refocus that energy on the things that you value the most. Your evaluation must be independent of external expectations. Why? Because you are the only one who lives your life, and only you can assign value to what you believe is most important.

How can we achieve perfection if we all have some physical and mental flaws? No one has the perfect body or mind. The most uncomplicated life is dynamic with many variables hard to understand. It is impossible to align everything in your life to achieve perfection. Think back to the last ten years of your life; how have things changed from year one to ten? Likely, there have been many changes and variables to contend with over that period. Life happens, and some things are out of our control. We search for perfection, but people—and life—are highly imperfect. TV shows and social media might lead us to believe some attain the ideal lives with perfect marriages and relationships, but that is not true—not even close.

Perfect and Performance

Large companies engineer performance ratings and appraisal systems based on perfection in too many dimensions. One company I worked for, a large corporation, measured our performance in four dimensions and fifty different competencies. What? How can one person try to meet those standards? We cannot, which brings us back to the paralyzing effects of perfect. I never viewed the vast number of dimensions and competencies in performance appraisals as helpful. It creates a competitive environment where people constantly try to outperform others instead of taking the broader view of teamwork. Supporting one another and co-creation provide more overall personal value and drive the organization closer to mission accomplishment. We need frameworks to work within, and we need boundaries, but make it simple and impactful for the individual.

Stop being the perfect employee. Trying to be the ideal employee makes your performance suffer, leading to people-pleasing. People-pleasing is terrible and kills your growth. You will have to put yourself out there at some point in your life/career. Likely, you will have all sorts of trepidations in anticipation of speaking the truth in your heart. Speak up and stand up, and do not be afraid to stand alone on issues that matter to you and are misaligned with your values.

Great leaders want alternative opinions and are not afraid to take criticism from below. You know you are in good company when you speak your truth quietly, professionally, and based on facts, and leaders accept it. Alternatively, anyone who continuously mutes your truth regardless of irrefutable facts is not your advocate. Get away from these types of people if at all possible.

Self-Leadership Is Not Perfect

Self-leadership is no exception to the rule. If self-leadership involves people and life, how can it be perfect? The answer is that we cannot get it perfect. Remember the leadership traits and values we discussed earlier? Just like business plans, they work on paper 100 percent of the time. But when we inject real life into our traits and values, it becomes an imperfect endeavor. It does not mean we retreat or give up; we only acknowledge that perfection is not attainable. You should always do your best to meet and exceed any standards you adopt or are organizationally accountable for upholding.

The best leaders are not perfect at self-leadership. Look at any president, prime minister, prominent corporation CEO, or professional sports coach, and you can find imperfections. Some are highly imperfect—they are people first. Likely, most of these folks realized that perfect is not realistic. Look no further than their decision-making for flaws. Indeed, some leaders are renowned for sound decision-making; however, they learn by making bad decisions. Decision-making is a good reality check for those who seek perfection. None of us can lay claim to perfect decision-making.

Pursue Excellence Instead of Perfection

"Perfection is not attainable, but if we chase perfection, we can catch excellence."

—Vince Lombardi

Pursuing mastery or excellence instead of perfection yields the best outcomes. We must ask what is more sustainable and effective, perfection or mastery/excellence? I believe if we take a hard look at perfection versus mastery/excellence, clearly pursuing master/excellence yields the best repeatable results. We are chasing mastery/excellence and knowing that it has many benefits, such as increased confidence despite small failures and more self-esteem, because you will not be so hard on yourself if you do not get it perfect.

Working toward mastery of anything is less stressful than trying to be perfect. Life includes many stresses, so why create unneeded stress for yourself? When pursuing excellence in any activity or field, it is essential to know the standards and expectations. Conversely, if you are making the standards and expectations, make them achievable. It is okay to stretch yourself but not set yourself up for failure by making unachievable standards and expectations. Think of setting goals in the "goal and stretch-goal mindset" (a sports analogy): a professional football team's goal is to win the next game. The stretch goal is to win the Super Bowl.

Sports analogies are helpful when coming to terms with imperfection being a part of life and work. Baseball players who hit three out of ten (.300 avg) trips to the plate are widely considered a success and exceptional hitters. Likewise, a quarterback who throws a 70 percent or better completion rate is outstanding. Those who compete at each sport's highest levels have less-than-perfect performances, even with the contrast. Still, each is considered a master in hitting and throwing, and their performances are effective.

Perfect performances are by exception. We can look at gymnastics. In the 1976 Olympics, Nadia Comaneci scored the first "10" on the uneven bars. At the time, no one thought a perfect 10 was achievable. When Comaneci stood next to the scoreboard, it read 1.00. Even the people who engineered the electronic scoring system did not think it possible or provide bandwidth for the chance someone would score a 10. Indeed, gymnasts strive for perfection. It is the odd sport where perfect was the goal. Over the years, the sport has changed from perfection to evolution, but you get the point here.

I remember watching an interview with Eddie Van Halen (EVH), the unquestionable king of the electric guitar. EVH talked about how his son's music teacher taught him the by-the-book music method. His son Wolfgang went home and reported the situation. EVH asked the music teacher not to approach teaching his son that way. His point was that it is music theory and not music fact. The lesson is that there are no perfect ways to learn music, and perfect gets in the way of creativity. EVH could not read sheet music and therefore did not create and arrange songs by the book. Nevertheless, EVH broke the rules and made some of the most memorable guitar licks in history because he was not worried about perfection.

We play how we practice in sports and other performances. If you are a person who strives for perfection and overthinks, then that is how you will show up on game day. Overthinking during practice carries over to the playing field. And overthinking leads to paralysis. I am sure you have heard the term *paralysis by analysis*. The saying succinctly describes what happens when we overthink.

Have you ever seen a quarterback hold the ball when he sees a wide-open receiver? You might think to yourself, *Why does he not pull the trigger?* The quarterback is overthinking. If you find yourself hesitating in your performance, go back to your practice habits and eliminate the overthinking.

Perfect Is the Enemy of Good

Perfect is an enemy. Have you ever heard that "perfect is the enemy of good or do not let perfect get in the way of good?" You have heard it many times, I am sure. The reality is that sometimes good is good enough. Read that again. Good is good enough. This does not mean settling for less or do not try your best.

Good enough does not mean half-ass. It means that in certain situations, good gets the job done. It means spending wisely the extra energy on other matters that require a higher level of attention.

All plans and theories are perfect on paper. Written plans represent the logical flow and pattern of events, but they usually fall short in the honest inclusion of people and outside-force imperfections. My personal experience is that planning is where most of the perfect expectations and concepts exist. Plans are excellent on paper, and I have seen plans overworked to the nth degree only to watch them fail in execution. The reason: planners and leaders expect the unattainable. They succumb to wishful thinking and fail to course-correct when the information and circumstances are staring them in the face.

"It's not a flaw, it's a handsome quirk."

—Richard Rheaume

It is not easy to overcome a perfectionist mindset. I would go so far as to say that it is impossible to completely rid your mind of it. I believe it is like other conditions that we must manage. I have days and instances where I digress into a perfectionist mindset, and in these cases, I must detach and realize that what I am doing is not constructive or effective. Moreover, striving for perfection and falling short time after time is a self-esteem killer. Living the life of an imperfect perfectionist is difficult at best and mentally destructive at worst.

In pursuing perfection, we lose sight of objectives and slow down. Indeed, perfect slows down everything. Most importantly, perfection slows thinking. If you have a penchant for perfection in each activity, analyze your thinking. It is akin to being in a phone booth. There are too many things to consider and over-thinking can paralyze. Instead, boil your thoughts down to the one or two most important variables that affect your thinking. Usually, this type of thinking allows us to think and invariably move faster; if something sticks out, we can adjust.

The human physical and mental makeup may have micro and macro flaws. People's learned behavior makes them imperfect. Yet people attempt to live, act, and speak perfectly every day, which is not likely to change. We can look at ourselves and others and stop expecting perfection. Likewise, we must stop being so upset with ourselves and others when we set perfect expectations and fail. Self-leadership and leaders are not an exception to perfect. In that light, perfect is not necessary; good is effective. Nothing is perfect.

CHAPTER SUMMARY

1. Believing in perfect is a dangerous proposition, as people represent the most flawed beings in the ecosystem.
2. See the world and embrace it as an imperfect place with ambiguity.
3. Strive for excellence and know when good is good enough.

CALL TO ACTION

1. In what areas of your life do you strive for perfection? Write them down.
2. Next, write down some areas in your life where you are doing well or achieving mastery/excellence.
3. Have you ever suffered in the pursuit of perfection? Recall specific experiences.
4. Begin, instead, to strive for mastery/excellence in your actions. Start by mapping out something you would like to achieve. Then work backward and outline all the steps necessary to accomplish it. Adjust your expectations along the way.

CHAPTER 11

SELF-CARE

Self-care has become a booming market commodity. It is a shift in behavior because most people do not take the time to care for themselves. It is understandable, though, as most people build a life that takes an inordinate amount of time just to stay ahead.

Unfortunately, I believe most people do not practice self-care because they did not learn it or see it in their parents early. As a result, folks get caught in sacrificing their needs for others. And while that is commendable, it lays waste to the person. The result is that we become tired, exhausted, and unable to stay physically and emotionally present. Moreover, we cannot care for and provide for others as we can when we are at our best.

"If you begin by sacrificing yourself for those you love, you will end by hating those to whom you have sacrificed yourself."

—George Bernard Shaw

But what exactly is self-care? There are many perspectives, but at its core, self-care is attending to your physical, emotional, and spiritual states. It is taking charge of your health. I do not believe anyone has a monopoly on the concept of self-care, so I would like to give you my version. Self-care is essential because if you do not take care of yourself, you are defeating your ability to lead yourself. Self-leadership requires your best self and the ability to be in the here and now.

Put Your Mask on First!

Boom! The importance of taking care of yourself first is so you can take care of others. That is right; you are number one—*numero uno*! You must make peace with the fact that you are the most important person when it comes to helping and serving others. If you are not at your best, then you cannot give others your best.

If you love others and you genuinely desire to serve them, take care of yourself. Your family, extended family, friends, colleagues, and work deserve your best you. Indeed, with so many people potentially seeking the best you, it is hella taxing, but guess what? It is damn well worth it. You will earn trust, and your character and competence will improve in the eyes of your circle.

Look at it this way: when you take care of yourself, you are taking care of others. It is a good way to think about it. How can you say no to treating yourself well if it benefits the ones you love? Sure, you may feel unnoticed or underappreciated—we all do at times. However, it is about what we can give to others; let the benefits to others be your payout for taking care of yourself.

Self-Care Is Important to Your Well-Being

Self-care must be intentional. Like other areas where we take inventory, we need to be on the lookout for blind spots. A blind spot is something you are doing in the physical, emotional, and spiritual areas that you are not aware of that is damaging you. For example, consistently consuming excessive alcohol, lack of sleep for days on end that is not purpose-driven, negative self-talk, and absence of a belief system. You are normalizing deviation, or you are suffering from standardization of deviation.

Again, many people dare greatly and pursue ventures that require long days and small hours of sleep. I cannot ask those folks to gear down and not pursue their passion. If long days and few hours of sleep are what is required to win, so be it. Just take caution here and read the previous paragraph again.

You will have to choose what is most important—work or family. The choice is a double-edged sword and a slippery slope at best. No easy decision here. Of course, we all believe our family is first; however, who is going to quit a high-paying job to take care of a sick family member when your salary or living funds the care of your loved one? Here is where sacrifice wins the day. We cannot discuss all scenarios in this text, but you get the point.

Make self-care intentional, especially if you are the long-hour and little-sleep individual. If your life is more pace and peak than work-life balance, perfect. Take time off on the back end. Do not roll right into the next three-week work bender that includes five cups of coffee and three naughty drinks each night just to cope. It is not sustainable. Detach from the work and do nothing related to your field. I suggest picking up a hobby that is high speed, low drag, i.e., easy to do and not much thinking. Give your head a rest. You will thank me after you are revived and refreshed. Your thoughts will clear, and the clutter of the work binge will subside. One way to ensure this happens is to schedule something with friends or family. The joint schedule is a forcing function to ensure you show up.

Save Yourself from Yourself

Some of us are late to the self-care space and concept. Having worked in the military and oil and gas, you would not hear many conversations about self-care among men. To be exact, I never heard one conversation about it. Maybe it was unspoken by way of a fishing, hunting, or game-day trip. Maybe it was doing nothing for the day. While a break from work, these activities might not provide *intentional* self-care. We need to go back to the pillars of physical, emotional, and spiritual self-care. I believe women might do a better job of self-care; however, I have observed they fall short as well.

There are indicators that you are not taking care of yourself: always looking for something to do, feeling anxious, experiencing emotional swings, and feeling guilty, to name a few. Your feelings and emotions play a critical role in your life, so it is essential to look after them. Feelings and emotions guide our opinion of the environment around us. We cannot leave the conversation without tying back emotions and feelings to self-control. If you remember our discussion of key attributes, you will remember how important bearing is. Regulating feelings and emotions directly aids us in maintaining our bearing in the most difficult of circumstances.

Put always looking for something to do, anxiety, emotional swings, and feeling guilty to use in another way. Try some simple things like staying involved when you feel stressed or anxious. You may have a feeling of flight but hanging out with friends or family may take those feelings away.

Do your best to stay away from self-pity. Self-pity cannot improve you or make any emotional issue go away. You are better than that, so stop it. Worry is the worst emotional grenade. Again, back to influence and control. We control little, and we influence less. Do not worry about things you cannot control. If you believe you have influence, make good decisions and use the influence wisely. You can control your actions and reactions to circumstances. Herein lies the secret sauce to emotional self-care, the cultivations of self-control, bearing, and how we react to things that happen. It takes time and repetition to improve self-control, bearing, and choosing to react or not. It is not easy, so stay the course.

Say if you are struggling with gravitation toward a particular subject, topic, behavior, or a social media platform, a good self-test is asking the priming question, *Is this improving me and moving me closer to my overall goal, or is it an obstacle to my goal?* Remember, even if it is noise, it takes up valuable space and energy.

Different Seasons—Different Care

We navigate different seasons in a lifetime. In turn, we should consider the right self-care. As we advance through the seasons, we naturally age. Our behaviors dictate the rate at which we age, and more physical self-care is required as we advance. Physical self-care can be whatever gets your body feeling good. Let's reflect on that for a second.

Feeling good can mean many things, such as being 100 percent healthy. Well, for those of us who have played sports through adolescence, high school, and possibly college, I am not sure if we are ever 100 percent because we accumulate injuries, and while injuries normally heal well, they creep up in later years.

The same applies to emotional health. People who have experienced trauma, post-traumatic stress disorder, or other events may never be 100 percent again. I believe it goes back to perfect, and we should maintain a sense of where we can realistically get to emotionally and physically. We can only do the best we can in our physical and emotional states. We age, and there are always problems, issues, and challenges in life that take a toll on our emotional well-being.

We can argue emotional self-care might garner top rank ahead of physical and spiritual. Although good physical condition and a belief system/spirituality strongly support emotional health. I cannot cite science here, but we can all agree that being in good physical shape and maintaining a belief system are strong pillars of emotional health. Everyone needs a religion, philosophy, or moral code to live by—it supports how you define and prioritize your values. In turn, your belief system supports your emotional health because it is what you believe in and influences how you live your life.

Self-Care Takes Repetition and Intention

Becoming proficient at self-care is tactical and strategic. We can do tactical exercises daily, yet we need to add intent for a strategic outcome. We need to determine where we have pain and what it takes to solve that pain. For instance, if a person struggles with a clouded mind and constantly pivots between personal life and work life, they may consider learning how to compartmentalize their thoughts and emotions. Likewise, if a person has a bad knee, they should get the right medical or orthopedic evaluation and then plan to take care of the physical injury.

Folks may get confused about their belief system or spirituality. They should seek the right person for council and ask the internal questions, *Why do I believe in this?* and *Am I committed?* For some folks, their belief system is a driver in life, and it serves as their spiritual self-care mechanism.

Make time for your self-care. I am going to call bullshit on the old saying, "I do not have time." The real answer is, "I did not make time," and we need to convert that into the positive response, "I will make time for me." Declare that you are going to make time for *YOU*. Start with fifteen minutes a day; that is enough to be intentional. Then move up to thirty minutes until you make time for one hour out of the day for only you. I can tell you that it works, and your ability to maintain self-care will improve.

My favorite and most effective techniques are meditation, breathing, and visualizing calm. Let's start with meditation. I find a quiet place to sit for thirty minutes. At the onset, the mind wanders; let it go as it will calm down. Do not fight it. Eventually, I get to a point where I only hear tinnitus and my breath; then, I am in relaxation mode.

I breathe normally until I calm down and then I start square breathing—commonly called box breathing. I breathe in for four counts, hold my breath for four counts, slowly exhale through my mouth for four counts, and repeat. While I breathe, I am meditating and visualizing calm. I usually think of myself walking in a forest in the early morning. It seems complicated and awkward initially, but over time, all three sync up. You may use this breathing technique for stressful situations or if you feel the onset of anxiety. I do the exercises in the morning or midday. I do not do it at night because I am planning the next day and there is too much anticipation to beat back. Do what works for you, make it intentional, and get the repetitions.

Set Physical, Emotional, and Spiritual Boundaries

Setting boundaries is one of the most effective ways to control a behavior. Likely, your parents or caregivers established boundaries for you as a child, right? There are all kinds of boundaries in life: speeding boundaries, legal boundaries, geographical boundaries, so why would we not establish some boundaries for self-care? There is no excuse; we should know our physical, emotional, and spiritual boundaries and set them accordingly.

For example, I limit myself to twelve to fourteen hours of work per day, and for the remainder, I will sleep, try a hobby, and practice self-care. Unless there is a deadline to meet, the work will be there tomorrow. Set a boundary on external noise like the news and politics. Ask yourself, *What is my return for investing so much mental space on this news topic and politics?* I am willing to bet not much. You absolutely have a right to have no opinion.

Self-Care Makes for Better Relationships

Practicing self-care regularly assists us in feeling better. When we feel better, we can give more to our relationships. In business, your network is your net worth. Personally, we need strong relationships with our family, relatives, and extended family. Although I am not saying self-care will solve family disputes at the yearly barbeque.

Your mental and emotional state projects to others. If you care deeply for others, then take care of yourself and pay attention to your relationships. Think of the last time you had a really bad day and took it out on your children, family, or others—that feels like shit. Hell of a hole to work out of. What if self-care helped manage your emotions? Practice self-care, think twice, and speak once. You will thank me.

Find a Way to Laugh

Laughing is the best medicine and a great way to reset your mood and mitigate the effects of stress. Think about the last time you laughed wholeheartedly—it changed your mood, and the good feeling lasted for some period. My mom always made the mood light when something heavy was going on with us. She knew if she could make us laugh, we would shake it off. Some things felt like big problems to us, but from her perspective, it was a life lesson we had to learn, and laughter could get us past it. She tried to soften grief's cruel education.

I remember being in Desert Storm and the Enemy Prisoner of War (EPW) camp we constructed came under artillery. It was not close enough to hit us but close enough to retreat. So, in fine military fashion, we retreated, but not before burning our armory. It was the most comical thing I have been around in a dangerous situation. We had enlisted Marines laughing and wooting, "Oorah! Hell yeah, let's get some," and Marines laughing at the officers who ordered the destruction of the armory. I was as serious as the front pew in church, but I had to laugh as well. I could not resist—it was both funny and bizarre. Dark humor and laughing in stressful situations are coping mechanisms. It is the result of anxiety, tension, and stress. Laughing and dark humor during difficult times down-regulates the primary causes —stress, anxiety, and tension. Some will not get it or will feel it is inappropriate; however, it is perfectly normal.

Let's close out this chapter by trying to improve your sense of humor. Get a joke book or share funny stories about yourself. Now please do not go to work next week, tell off-color jokes, and use inappropriate content after reading this book. That is not the intent here. Note: when you laugh or joke, please make sure you are laughing with folks and not at them. There is no need to create offense at the expense of others. Lastly, learn to laugh at yourself.

I trust you will consider self-care and take onboard some of the concepts discussed in this text. You are important to many people, so we want you to be at your absolute best. Taking care of yourself physically is important; it is essential to your quality of life. Moreover, physical problems can lead to mental issues. Using self-care to regulate our emotions is crucial to maintaining a positive outlook on life and critical to our interpersonal relationships.

CHAPTER SUMMARY

1. Self-care is necessary to balance physical, mental, and spiritual health.
2. You are the most important person; take care of yourself first so you can take care of others.
3. Effective self-care requires intention and repetition.

CALL TO ACTION

1. Determine in what areas of your life you are successfully caring for yourself and in what areas you might need a little more work.

2. Research the benefits of self-care to acquire a deeper understanding of its importance.

3. Find what forms of self-care work best for you. Identify what works and what does not.

4. Make time to conduct self-care. Start by scheduling fifteen minutes a day and eventually work up to a full hour if possible.

CHAPTER 12

SELF-LEADERSHIP IS HARD

You Will Fail—Keep Moving!

Do you accept that self-leadership is hard? Are you committed to a lifelong journey of self-leadership improvement despite setbacks? In any great endeavor, the road is long. What we do with the time between starting and finishing is what counts. Earlier in the book, we discussed daring greatly. Developing self-leadership is a daring feat where you must make decisions about the traits and values you intend to cultivate.

It would be best if you committed to staying sovereign on your most important values. Setbacks are going to occur in every part of your life. You have overperformed and underachieved if you manage a lifetime and career without setbacks. Please read that again because it is the truth, and that truth may hurt.

We must endeavor to push ourselves past our imagined boundaries. Lead yourself further than you can see, and you will find out where your actual boundaries exist. Failure is imminent in all things. The degree to which we fail is mostly within our control if we honestly own our situation.

Personal accountability is critical to leading ourselves, especially when we fail. Taking ownership of our failures is a growth mindset and a sign of maturity. Everyone can lead themselves effectively if they are committed to it, so do not give up when it gets hard or failure occurs because you have everything you need to succeed!

What Does Failure Mean?

Let's start with a few different definitions and perspectives on failure. The most common description of failure is lack of success. This definition paints failure as a zero-sum outcome. You had success, or you did not. Another definition is to fall short of expectations. It is as if the folks who made these definitions left no room for the abstract part of failure. Let's be clear: failure is something that happens; it is not a person. Read that again—if you fail, failure does not define you. There is an immense amount of feedback and opportunity in failure. Failure validates your weaknesses and provides feedback where you need work. Failure can unlock tenacity, more discipline, and resilience.

Self-leadership is the hardest thing a person can undertake, and failure is almost inevitable. Life is full of personal disappointment, obstacles, emotions, temptations, and the opportunity to fail is around each corner. If you want to be successful, you will need to fail often. Some say, "increase your failure rate." Read that again. If failure is imminent and necessary for growth, we must learn how to manage failure effectively.

It does not mean you have to fail intentionally; that does not make sense. It goes back to stretching your boundaries. Life and business are not like school, where you study and then test your subject-matter knowledge. You get the test first in life and business, and you learn from your failures. But how we handle failure is the measure of self-leadership. There is no choice but to see failure as an opportunity. When we learn to see failure as a way to improve, we quickly take back control and keep moving. Handling failure takes practice and perspective.

I have found that developing a short memory and cultivating the ability to compartmentalize work best. Develop a short memory when a failure occurs. What does that mean? In simple terms, you develop the ability to forget failure quickly. You forget about the sting, the regret, and the shame often associated with failure. Instead, you focus on how you can learn from the failure.

The first step is to look within and ask the tested priming questions. *What was in my control? What did I influence, and what could I have done better with my willingness and ability to pursue this goal or task?* The idea is to quickly separate *how* I can learn from the failure (constructive) instead of *why* I feel bad about the failure (destructive).

The mental separation is compartmentalization. It is no easy task to compartmentalize failure. We are human; we have feelings and emotions, and we have been cultured to believe anything short of perfect and winning is bad. Yes, everyone has feelings; get over it. Indeed, the goal is to win, but we must acknowledge that on the way to winning, we will experience small failures. No one wins everything all the time for their entire life.

Coping with Failure

The next time you fail, make two columns on a piece of paper and write down the constructive part of failure first and then the destructive. Always give the positive first billing; this builds a positive mindset because you will see the constructive first. It is part of anchoring your mind to think in a certain way. Segregating the thoughts on paper creates a mental picture of the constructive and destructive aspects of failure. You can then compartmentalize the failure mentally. Keep doing this until you can do it in your mind. If you make an honest attempt at this, you will learn about yourself. The next step is to let yourself forget the destructive part of failure. Next, do not give two shits about what others think. They do not live your life or earn your living, so why care so much? Stop that—now!

Not everyone copes with failure in the same way, nor should we expect it. Find what works for you. I use self-talk and compartmentalization. I have found this technique to be the most useful to me. You might try the same or other methods. If you experience an inordinate amount of anxiety because of failure, reach out to a trusted ally, exercise, or meditate on something positive. If you fail at a task, set some boundaries and processes to get back on track.

The "self-talk and compartmentalization" structure is an excellent way to start toward meaningful repetitions at a given task. You can apply the self-talk and compartmentalization structure to your mental thinking as well. Make your best attempt to think of one thing at a time. When you are at work, think of work things. You must learn to drive out all other thoughts. When you get home, leave work at the door, which is difficult at first because it is a part of us, and we spend more time there than at home. Also, the more responsibility we have, the more it will weigh on our consciousness. Still, the best way to start the compartmentalization process is to segregate work and home. You will thank yourself for doing it.

Let go of failure and stay present. I have seen folks (including myself) carry failure like a smelly blanket. Why do we do this type of thing? Self-loathing maybe—but carrying around failure did not make me feel any better and did not allow me to move on quickly or learn from the failure. I have observed the same in others who carry around failure, and it is hard to watch. It is okay to be your own worst critic; however, you must manage it in a way that improves you. Again, failure is not a part of you; it occurs because of our willingness, ability, and the effects of outside forces.

Wear Your Failures with Pride

I have learned to wear my failures with pride. If I give an honest effort and approach my goal's tasks with all my willingness and ability, then there is nothing to be ashamed of if I fail. To have tried and failed is better than not to have given the effort to try at all. Regret is a hell of a thing. I believe most of us carry some regret, but it is not a healthy thing.

To regret trying something your heart desires because you are afraid of failure is dreadful. If something is so important to you that you will regret not doing it, then you absolutely must go for it. If you fail at it, so what? Try again. Many of the most extraordinary people have failed multiple times. Trying hard things numerous times can cause great suffering. In that light, failure is a benefit because suffering, setbacks, and hardship build resilience.

Anything Worth Doing Has Failure in the Ingredients

I spent eight years implementing technology for a Fortune 100 company. There were many failures along the way, and quitting would have been easy. Instead, I spent eight years developing and deploying the technology and learned about failure, resilience, and feedback. The thing that drove me was the fear of failing at the endpoint. In my head and my heart, I had to see it through. Although I learned more about failure, a minor failure would not tamper with my determination. Honestly, I was obsessed with accomplishing what I knew was possible.

When you know in your heart that something is possible and you are determined, you will start to block out some of the noise because your focus sharpens on what matters, and that is the next milestone or next critical task. Blocking out the noise also means you will not think twice about a minor failure and will learn to repurpose failure to your advantage. The mindset changes from falling short on this or not meeting expectations here to: *This is what we learned and what we can improve on. This is how we will do it differently moving forward.* We failed many times in eight years of implementing the technology. We used failure to learn, and at the end of the day, the technology saved the company millions of dollars—all resulting from learning from failure.

Your Perception of Failure Matters

Part of the problem is how we perceive failure and celebrate success. We are cultured to believe anything less than success is a failure, which is the wrong approach. A better way to approach failure is to learn from it. Failure is necessary for personal growth. There can be no significant growth without failure.

> *"One day, in retrospect, the years of struggle will strike you as the most beautiful."*
>
> —Sigmund Freud

Overcoming failure requires resilience, and resilience only comes with meaningful repetition of hardship, suffering, or struggle. Like doing manual labor builds callouses, hardship creates resilience by indoctrinating you to certain conditions. More experience with difficulties and failure gives us mental callouses. None of us wakes up to pursue suffering unless we know it is part of the plan to get what we want.

Some people in this world have no choice but to suffer as others impose it on them. Go to a developing country, and you will see suffering everywhere, but suffering may be only a tiny part of the existence of the people there. Why? The answer is that they have built resilience. It is all about the perspective you give to suffering. Do not underestimate the value of struggle. People say there is much to learn at rock bottom. Indeed, being in the depths of a problem or life circumstance is heavy, and there is much to learn.

I have learned there is immense value in the struggle. The will to keep struggling develops grit—the steadfastness of mind. Seek the hard things that provide the struggle. I like to say I live in between the g's in the struggle. Never relenting on the things I am committed to and desire, though there is a significant struggle to get there, constantly embroiled in some struggle. Once I accomplish what I am working on, I look for another challenge and struggle.

Remember that you are never alone in failure. Everyone has failed at something. And someone has likely failed at the things you have failed at too. Ruminating about failures has no value. Worrying about failure is the most worthless activity we can undertake. There is no learning, no growth, and only destructive mental outcomes.

Continued worry will affect your actions, decisions, and choices. It is imperative that you make peace with what you control and influence. We control some things, and others we have no control over. We have little actual influence on most situations. Where we have firm control and influence, failure should be minimal. Just realize that most conditions are beyond our control, and outside forces unknown to us can significantly influence outcomes. Failure is necessary for growth, and in that light, it is essential for self-leadership development. The key is to embrace the constructive side of failure, where we learn our faults, and we can improve them.

The Secret Sauce

Everyone wants a performance hack, a shortcut; ultimately what they really want is the secret to perform like the top performers. I have given you one part of the secret in this book already—hard work. Although hard work alone is just that, hard work, there is another component to the secret sauce—Grit. So, what makes up grit? There may be many definitions in circulation, but I would like to give you mine. Grit is passion, perseverance, and doing things with intention. How do we cultivate grit, or is it something instantaneous we can recall at will? It depends. Have you ever wanted something so bad you couldn't stop thinking about it? Did you ever get up and you automatically think of the one thing you are pursuing and how it is difficult, and everyone says you cannot do it? But you keep going because your desire and hunger overpowers any outside influence. That is grit. Fighting up a hill with fury in the face of overwhelming odds—that is grit. Doing a few more reps or sets while working out when the pain comes—that is grit. Playing a guitar until your fingers bleed—that is grit. Dissect any of the previous examples and you will find hard work, perseverance, and doing things with intention. Prove me wrong. The last thing is to manage your focus on top of that and you have grit with intention.

Your level of passion for a goal or dream will drive the amount of grit you are able to demonstrate. The more grit you possess, the more likely you are to achieve a goal or dream. Maintaining grit is not easy if you do not truly want something. Does grit come naturally? Grit is developed through experience, yet some people are predisposed to act with grit. Grit can be inherited; apples do not fall far from the tree. Likewise, an experience can ignite the will to cultivate grit. Think about the athlete who gets cut or told they don't measure up, and then the next year they come back and dominate. Wherever you observe people accomplishing big goals, it is guaranteed grit was part of their journey.

If you want to develop grit, examine the things in your life that you desire more than anything else. Increase your effort at those few things you truly love. As you cultivate grit in those areas, it will rub off in other areas of your life. I guarantee it. You do not have to be gritty at everything, just those things that matter to you most.

CHAPTER SUMMARY

1. Failure and struggle are part of the self-leadership journey.
2. Your perception of failure has a constructive or destructive anchor.
3. Struggle builds resilience.
4. Develop a short memory, keep moving and learning.

CALL TO ACTION

1. Start by examining two or three failures you have experienced during your life. This could be a failure in a relationship, on a project, or during an assignment. How did you respond to each failure? What did you learn from them? Did you allow the failure to define you? Have you carried your failure with you?

2. Is there something you have been unwilling to do or try because of the fear of failing? Make a list of actions you would take if failure were no longer an option. Once you successfully shift your perspective on failure, give that list a try!

3. The next time you receive negative feedback or criticism, ask yourself what you can learn from that experience. Rather than internalizing the negative, endeavor to transform it into a positive.

4. Remember, above all else, that not everything is happening *to* you. It is happening *for* you. Take advantage of that fact!

CONCLUSION

Self-leadership is not a high-wire act; it is doing the basics well and operating within a leadership framework. When we lead ourselves, sure enough, we lead others more effectively. We cannot lead others effectively if we do not commit to leading ourselves first. And we cannot lead effectively where we have not walked. These are not mere maxims, but leadership facts—proved time and time again throughout history. Personal accountability and responsibility comprise the umbrella of all leadership frameworks. We cannot effectively lead ourselves if we do not adopt a leadership framework consisting of traits and values.

Beyond traits and values lie other important ingredients to self-leadership, such as self-trust, self-belief, commitment, and discipline. We must develop strong self-trust, self-belief, and commitment. These three values are the foundation of discipline. And without discipline, we will never realize our fullest potential.

Discipline does not cost any money, although it does require uncommon effort. Discipline carries the day when you are striving to meet your personal expectations and big goals. Like discipline, the courage to stay sovereign on the things that matter will set you apart from others and strengthen your self-leadership abilities. Staying sovereign to your values serves notice to people and organizations that you are not okay with the status quo group thinking and decision-making. Do not give up on what you believe is right. Whether it is raining, snowing, or sunny, north is north. Remember, nothing is perfect, so do not place an undue burden on yourself to be perfect. No one has done it yet.

Doing your job is always the best approach to work and your career. The best way to get what you want is to work against your own expectations and do not succumb to the over-ambitious stereotype. It may support short-term progression, but it never works out well in the long run.

Work hard, make a plan, and have career discussions when you are truly ready and know what you want. Someone will notice your value and lift you up. If not, you are in the wrong organization. Also, remember that promotion comes in many forms. Take the time out for yourself to rejuvenate. You deserve the best you! Besides, others are counting on you, so why not give them your best self—day in and day out? You will notice your relationships change when you start to take care of yourself.

Through a systematic and compartmentalized approach to self-leadership, we can cultivate our leadership character. *Lead*

You is about creating personal accountability by having the honest conversation people need to have with themselves, and realizing leadership starts with learning a leadership framework and doing the basics with excellence. It is for aspiring leaders, journeymen, and people who may have had a setback and are stuck in the leadership trenches. Before you accept the challenge to dedicate time and effort to your personal leadership journey, let's test with some essential priming questions.

There are six questions to answer if you seek to lead yourself in the most effective way possible:

1. What values are nonnegotiable no matter the circumstances?
2. Do you have the grit to make disliked decisions?
3. Are you willing to embrace self-awareness and the demands of self-leadership?
4. Are you willing to take accountability for your actions and decisions?
5. Are you willing to struggle for self-improvement?
6. Are you willing to build and protect trust with yourself and others?

If you have answered yes to all the questions above, you are ready to pursue a self-leadership journey of excellence. If you are a journeyman or you have had a setback, the same applies, as it is never too late to sail in the right direction.

The road to effective self-leadership is long, and it is not a linear process. There will be many pitfalls along the way. Tighten your belt and accept the challenge. If you study the traits and values in the book, adopt a personal self-leadership framework, use the perspectives and anecdotes from this text and other trustworthy sources, and use the calls to action included herein to kickstart your journey, I am confident you can accept the hardship of self-leadership. You can do it; keep going!

Let us know your thoughts on our method and how we can support your leadership needs moving forward. Please go to leadyoubook.com.

ABOUT THE AUTHOR

BOBBY HARRINGTON is the founder of the Rubicon Course of Action (COA) Immersive Leadership Development company, specializing in performance programs and immersive-leadership development events. He has practiced leadership in sports, martial arts, the military, private business, and a Fortune 100 oil and gas company. Bobby has taught leadership in twenty-four different countries with thirteen languages. His work focuses on people in leadership, team design, and technical innovation leadership. He earned a degree in Intelligence Studies and International Relations later in life. Bobby is a United States Marine Corps Desert Shield/Desert Storm Gulf War veteran and lives in Texas with his wife and family.

My grandfather Ernest Harrington, a Navy veteran with WWI service.

My father Robert W. Harrington, a Navy, Army Air Corps, and US Air Force veteran of WWII, Korea, and Vietnam.

My father Robert W. Harrington convening staff and civilians for a special project overseas.

Corporal Robert M. Harrington, 29 Palms MCAGCC

Lance Corporal Robert M. Harrington training in Okinawa before Desert Storm.

Lance Corporal Robert M. Harrington, Camp Geiger
Marine Combat Training (60 Gunner Pit)

Lance Corporal Robert M. Harrington, Camp Geiger Marine Combat Training (lost twenty pounds in thirty days)

Lance Corporal Robert M. Harrington, Desert Storm—
Enemy Prisoner of War (EPW) camp

Lance Corporal Robert M. Harrington, Camp Geiger
(middle of a thirty-mile hump with full gear)

Lance Corporal Robert M. Harrington Camp Geiger, Marine Combat Training (end of one of many endless days)

ACKNOWLEDGMENTS

I must start by thanking my wife and love, Angella. From the moment I started with the idea of formalizing my thoughts on self-leadership, you have been supportive. You never complained during the countless hours I spent writing and editing. Thank you for the continued encouragement.

Thank you, Mom and Dad, for raising me and always teaching me the value of hard work, perseverance, and to always finish. Dad, I learned so much from your selfless sacrifice, and Mom, you are still the toughest person I have ever known.

Thank you, Laura Lee and Ethan, you have always made me proud to be your Dad, and thanks for listening to all my speeches on leadership. Keep going and keep working hard for your dreams.

I want to thank my brother and sister Travis and Melisa for always supporting me and acting as my soundboard.

A big, green, amphibious thanks to the gritty and steadfast leaders of the United States Marine Corps past, present, and future. No one does leadership better than the Marines. Thank you for all the valuable and profound lessons on leadership during my tour of duty. The lessons have stuck with me to this day, and I continue to practice the traits and principles taught to every Marine regardless of rank. Oorah!

Thanks, Jocko Willink and Leif Babin, for the book *Extreme Ownership*; it came at the right time to give me a new perspective on ownership and accountability.

Thanks to Marcus Luttrell and the book *Lone Survivor*. Reading about you not quitting in the face of overwhelming odds and doing your absolute best gave me a new perspective on performance.

Thank you, Sean Roach, for your friendship, book guidance, and for introducing me to Scribe!

Thanks to everyone on the Scribe team who helped me so much. Special thanks to Katherine, my editor; Sophie, Chas, Hussein, and Chelsea, the greatest cover designer I could ever imagine. A very special thanks to Emily for challenging me to write with the "bottom of the truth" in mind. Special thanks to Jevon for putting people first and making Scribe an awesome culture and company to cocreate with. Well done!

DOWNLOAD YOUR FREE GIFTS

Just to say thanks for buying and reading my book,
I would like to give you a few free bonus gifts,
no strings attached.

To download now, visit
www.leadyoubook.com/Freegifts

*I appreciate your interest in my book, and
I value your feedback as it helps me improve future versions.
I would appreciate it if you could leave a review on
Amazon.com with your invaluable feedback.*

Thank you!